A Place To Belong

A Place To Belong

The True Story of a Teen Mom,
a Humbling Leadership Journey,
and a House Called Hope

Lisa Steven

with Susy Flory

credo
house publishers

Lisa Steven weaves her very personal experience of being a teen mom with the lives of various teen moms to tell the story of Hope House. Over a twenty-year journey of personal and spiritual growth, Lisa discovered God's faithfulness to provide for her own needs while serving a population desperate to be the best moms possible. Whatever challenge you face, Lisa's story of Hope House will empower you to say yes to God and watch Him work!

—Elisa Morgan
Speaker, Author, *You Are Not Alone*
Co-Host of the syndicated radio show Discover the Word (discovertheword.org) and God Hears Her (godhearsher.org) and President Emerita, MOPS International (now The MoMCo mops.org/themomco)

If you ever wonder if God sees the lost and rejected and abused, if you ever wonder if his heart is moved by their suffering, if you need solid evidence that He is with us and for us and will move heaven and earth to rescue his own, look no further. The story of Hope House and Lisa Steven in *A Place to Belong* is packed full of proof of God's kindness and goodness and His ability to work miracles big and small to let the least know they are infinitely loved. That includes you, too.

—Michele Cushatt
Speaker, Executive Coach, Author, *A Faith That Will Not Fail*

When Lisa Steven discovered that she was a teen mom, she heard someone whisper, "That's the end of her life." NOTHING could have been further from the truth. Her story of healing with the help of family and faith in God is a page turner. The story of how she grew to establish a place to belong will touch your life and give you hope. When I first met Lisa, I was amazed at her passion for teenage mothers. In the past years I have marveled at the work she has done to give these children of God and their children a "Place to belong." As you read, you too will marvel at God's faithfulness, and miracles along the way. EVERBODY needs a place to belong and a copy of this book.

—Ken Davis
Author, Speaker, Comedian and Founder of SCORRE Speaker Academy

A Place to Belong is an incredible story written from the true life heartbreak and success journey of the author, Lisa Steven. Lisa's vulnerable storytelling and her ability to weave real life circumstances into valuable life lessons is what inspired me. Lisa shares how God worked in her life story, and she shares in detail how it required her to lean into those God placed in her life to assist along the way. This book brought to life Romans 8:28, "And we know that in all things God works for the good of those who love him, who have been called according to his purpose." Guaranteed, you will be inspired.

—Sherri Crandall
Vice President of Global Ministries and Leadership Experience for
The MomCo by MOPS International

Lisa bravely shares her journey from a teen mom herself to executive director of Hope House, a program she started that empowers teen moms. Her story of trusting God's powerful provision in hard times and remarkable stories of teen moms who've been impacted through the ministry are strong testimony of what God does through those who are willing to say yes to doing His work. I wholeheartedly recommend this book to anyone seeking an uplifting, faith-filled journey that will leave them inspired and encouraged.

—Jeannie Blackmer
Author of *MomSense: A Common-Sense Guide to Confident Mothering*

Dedication

People often say that God will equip those He calls, and my journey with Hope House certainly exemplifies this. I strongly believe that one of the ways He equips the called is by surrounding them with the most amazing people to assist them on their journey. Without my incredibly wise, loyal, and steadfast husband, John, Hope House would never have existed. It is with a truly grateful heart that I dedicate this book to my husband and my children, who had to listen to far too many Hope House conversations around the dinner table growing up but always supported their parents in this call (our very first donation to Hope House was a $1.00 bill from our then ten-year-old son, Nate). John, Johnny, Nate, and Heather, this journey and this book wouldn't exist without you!

To Sharron Neufeld and our incredible prayer team, who have covered us in prayer since before Hope House began. Your dedicated prayers have gone before us and cleared the way for all that we are and will be.

In addition, I want to acknowledge my deep gratitude to Pastor John Tellis and Lisa Schlarbaum, along with my husband, John, for encouraging (perhaps even exhorting) me to write this book when I felt way too shy to attempt it! You made it clear that this book was a part of the calling and a piece of the kingdom building work of Hope House!

To Bill and Donna Wehner, you made this book a reality. From the many, many hours Donna spent writing a first draft so long ago to Bill's determination to invest in our story—this book reflects your dedication to Hope House and our teen mamas.

To every single staff member who has ever worked at Hope House—you have poured your heart, talent, and passion into our teen moms and children, breaking the cycle of poverty for countless moms and children and literally loving each mom and child to Christ while doing so!

To every volunteer and donor who has invested time and treasure into Hope House—your love and generosity continue to astonish me. It would simply be impossible to name every volunteer who has cherished a teen mom or her child and every donor who has invested not just their treasure, but their faith and belief, into our teen mamas, but please know that *your names are written on my heart and on theirs.* This story is *our* story, and I am so incredibly humbled and grateful that God has brought each of you into our Hope House family.

To Susy Flory, who wrote this book with me—it is your incredible giftedness and profound patience over the past six years that have finally brought this book to life. Thank you for helping me shape it from twenty years of journals and countless stories of God's provision into what it is today—I couldn't have done this without you, and that is a fact!

To my three beautiful granddaughters—you are my world, and I love you to the moon and back! To my two beautiful sisters—you are the only two people in the world who have shared the entirety of my life with me. I look up to you, respect you, and love you so much. You are my heroes!

To my Bible study girls—thank you for walking through this life with me and pointing me back to Jesus at every turn! To our Friday night small group—thank you for allowing me to just be me and for making life an adventure!

To every board member who has ever served on our board, and particularly to every single board chair—this ministry would not exist without your willingness to accept the call to leadership. You are my most trusted advisors. You *always* keep this ministry focused on Christ. I admire and respect each of you more than you will ever know.

Finally, to every teen mom whom I have ever had the privilege of loving—this book is for you. It wasn't possible to name each of you individually, as there are so many of you now, but each one of you holds an incredibly special place in my heart. You are so brave, strong, beautiful, determined, and smart. You are incredible mamas. You inspire me every single day. Thank you for allowing me to be a part of your journey!

Contents

Foreword

"Well, her life is over now!" These words were burned into my memory forever. Hearing second hand the reaction of a friend's mother—a somewhat gleeful reaction, I might add—to my predicament as a teen mother-to-be was devastating. But it was also motivating.

I was oh-so-young and very naive, but I was also lucky. I had a supportive family. I had good grades and an academic future. But getting pregnant at the age of sixteen gave me something I didn't know I had: a deep well of determination to do the best I could for my daughter by forging our own unique path. I was motivated to prove my friend's mother wrong. Eventually, I did.

Very few girls in my situation are as fortunate. Lisa's stories of some of these girls are heartbreaking. They are stories of trauma, abuse, and abandonment. But they are also stories of determination, which, as Lisa shares, is what most teen moms have in common.

A Place to Belong is a hugely important book, telling the origins and development of Hope House Colorado, a community designed to help teen moms embrace their determination with multiple levels of support. It is filled to the brim with unbelievable acts of generosity, as well as stories of teen moms and their children fighting past their limitations and trauma to achieve the miracle of self-sufficiency. But the stories presented in this book, I'm sure, have only scratched the surface of the daily miracles that seem to follow Lisa and Hope House.

I was a witness, and a lucky participant, in one tiny miracle.

I was invited to speak at a women's leadership conference in Boulder, Colorado. I'm sure the conference organizers were hoping to tap into the professional learnings I had gleaned as a woman in the workplace, with perhaps some juicy insight into my days at Google. But for some reason I felt called to talk about the origins of my journey into adulthood, which was as a teen mom. I flew my daughter out from college to meet me for the conference, hear the talk, and spend a weekend together afterward.

It had been the first time I had publicly spoken about my journey, and I had no idea how it would be received. To my delight/relief, there was a lovely positive response from the audience. But what I couldn't imagine in my wildest dreams was what happened as my daughter and I emerged from the conference room into the lobby: a Lisa-miracle is the best way I can put it.

Standing by, patiently waiting for me to emerge, was a long line of beautiful young women with smiles beaming from ear to ear. Lisa was at the forefront and quickly introduced herself, and then she turned to say that she had brought these teens to the conference to learn about leadership. Teen moms, of course. And to their shock and surprise, there I was on stage talking about my journey as a teen mom.

It was a moment of pure joy and connection and beauty; they touched me to my core, and I'm sure my story served as a beacon to show that they, too, could do it. It was as if the entire conference conspired to create this moment.

Lisa and I have stayed connected through the years, and I am always excited to hear about the developments and progress of Hope House. I consider her to be a friend and a model of true and pure devotion. Her mission is clear, and what I value most from her book is the message that we can always make things happen, no matter the humble beginnings and the statistics that suggest it's not possible. For teen moms, for Hope House, for each of us.

Julie Clow, PhD
Author, *The Work Revolution*
Former high-level roles with Google and Chanel
Talent, Leadership, and Culture Advisor

Alondra with her son, Aiyden, 2013

1

Who, Me?

God loves you so much and has a plan for your life!

PARAPHRASE OF JEREMIAH 29:11

What if it's true that God chooses the least qualified, least likely people to do the most extraordinary things?

What if you just might be one of those people?

Maybe you have a thought you can't get out of your head or a deep concern for something or someone in particular that you can't shake. Maybe you feel like God might even be asking you to *do* something about it, but in your head you're thinking, *Yeah, but that would be crazy! I'm just . . .*

. . . a stay-at-home mom

. . . a college dropout

. . . a grocery store clerk

Or maybe you have the big career everyone envies, but you can't shake the feeling that there's something more—but buying into God's plan for you would cost you so much.

What if God really is tapping you on the shoulder—and what if you were to say yes?

I watch in astonishment as Alondra, now twenty-four years old, crosses the stage in a graduation ceremony at Metro State University's King Hall. This sweet teen mom looks lovely in a new pink dress, her long, dark hair pulled up. She doesn't appear to be nervous, though this momentous occasion has my own stomach doing flip-flops.

God, I can't believe you made my dream come true.

Alondra stops center stage and turns to watch her little boy, Aiyden, saunter across the stage with his usual confident air, seemingly unaware that all eyes are on him. Aiyden is eight years old and sporting his first suit, his hair pulled up in a man-bun after he demanded to grow it long. He clutches a rose in one hand and a gold pin in the other, and when he reaches his mom she bends down so that he can attach the pin to her dress in the traditional ceremonial welcome for every new nurse entering the profession.

Mother and son turn to the audience with irrepressible matching grins, searching for our faces in the crowd. They might be the only two in the building with no biological family members present for the ceremony, but an entire row of Hope House staff and volunteers jumps up from their seats with cheers and shouts for Alondra and Aiyden.

I am smiling and crying at the same time. She has come such a long way since she came to Hope House at age seventeen, literally carrying nothing but her one-year-old son. Alondra was homeless, scared, and alone, but she has finally found a place to belong. My heart is so full of pride and joy for this beautiful girl, who has officially broken the cycle of poverty for her son and for future generations as well.

Such a long way, and so many barriers for Alondra to overcome. Such a long way for *me*, too, since that day when I, at the age of seventeen, was sitting outside a clinic with my boyfriend, trying to figure out what to do with the unexpected news that we were pregnant.

Nothing will ever be the same, I thought. I was right.

I was once a girl like Alondra trying desperately to climb out of a chaotic and difficult childhood. I, too, became a mother before becoming an adult, and it would have been easy to believe the statistics that said I would fail as a mom, that my teenage marriage wouldn't last, that I wouldn't amount to much. Yet God doesn't see things the way the rest of the world does. After all, He chose Mary, just a teenage girl herself, to be the mother of Jesus. Mary was probably even younger than I was when she gave birth to the Savior of the world. But she was wise, and her ready willingness to submit to God and be obedient to His call continues to inspire me.

I know that, right now, somewhere out there is a scared and lonely teen mom curled up with her baby and desperate for help. Her heart is hurting and her mind reeling. *How can I go on? What am I going to do next?*

I believe that God is kneeling right there next to that girl, whispering in her ear, *Just hold on. I'm sending my people.*

I also believe that at the exact same moment He is standing right there next to you, whispering in *your* ear: *I have something for you to do.*

All you need to do now is say yes, and then hold on for the ride of your life. I know because I did that once—me, a very

unlikely girl whom God somehow chose for an extraordinary
assignment. It was an assignment I would have to say yes to before
He could begin teaching me, equipping me, and surrounding me
with extraordinary people to help me carry it out.

In over twenty years of ministry to teen mothers and their
children, I have often been humbled by their strength, their grit,
and their determination to overcome incredible barriers in order
to build stable lives for their children. I am convinced that teen
moms can change the world, breaking the cycle of poverty and
despair, if only given a chance. This is their story, and it's mine,
too.

From left to right: Chris, Lisa, Jenny, and Marla, 1972

2

Too Little to Be a Grownup

You keep track of all my sorrows.

PSALM 56:8A NLT

When I think back to my childhood, what I most remember is walking on eggshells. I never felt completely safe because I never knew when the fighting or yelling would start. From the outside we looked like a typical middle-class family, but situational poverty and an erratic father who couldn't hold down a job was our normal. I was the oldest of four, with two younger sisters and a brother, and, in my mind, I was their chief protector.

My first real memory is of my parents fighting at dinnertime. I was maybe four or five; the twins, Marla and Chris, were three; and Jenny was a toddler in a highchair. A pot of tomato soup sat on the table, and for some reason Dad was mad about the soup. There was yelling. Then he picked up the pot of hot soup and flung it across the table at Mom.

My first reaction was to scramble back from the table, pulling Marla and Chris by their tiny wrists into the next room.

Safer there. I was too short to get Jenny out of her highchair and had to leave her wailing in the chaos.

I don't remember how that particular episode ended. These visuals are fuzzy, like a faded black-and-white photograph from a dusty album. The emotions are still with me, though—alarm, fear, confusion—and the absolute urgency of protecting my younger siblings.

My dad held a number of jobs, but he always seemed to either quit them or lose them. He was an incredibly intelligent man with a scientific mind and a deep curiosity about the natural world. For college he attended the prestigious School of Mines, where he studied geology, but he never completed his degree. As with most things, he just couldn't seem to finish.

When Dad was out of work, my siblings and I were bystanders at intense screaming matches about borrowing money from one set of grandparents or the other—typically from my mom's parents, who were better off and who mostly hated my dad.

Nothing about my childhood was orderly or safe, except church. My dad's parents went to a Lutheran church where my grandma was the secretary. Later my mom took us to a neighborhood church, Holy Cross Lutheran, and I loved it. There was an order to everything, a sense of quietness and reverence. I always knew what to expect and grew to love the cadence and rhythm of the services. I figured that God lived there and that he brought his order, peace, and strength.

Unfortunately, God didn't seem to live at my house. Only at church, and maybe at Grandma's. The interesting thing about having a difficult childhood is that the happy memories are so bright. Even the colors are sharper. My dad loved camping and fishing, and I remember his smile as the sun shimmered on the water, making sparkles. I remember the plastic smell when we put the tent up and the smoky scent of the campfire. I can still hear the sound of my dad laughing when we roasted marshmallows and one fell off the stick and into the fire, where it puffed up into bright flame and then shrank back down into what looked like a black, foaming lump of coal.

I remember hiding in the garden one time, back in the cornstalks, with my sister Marla. Dad couldn't find us anywhere, and we hid for an hour, giggling and cupping our hands over our mouths, trying not to make any noise. By the time he found us, he was so worried and mad that he wanted to give us a spanking. But Marla hung onto the arms of her chair so tightly that, when he tried to pick her up, the whole chair came with her. We started giggling again. My dad couldn't resist and dissolved into laughter, too.

Shiny, sparkly moments woven through the difficult, dark ones.

Once, on a visit to the food stamp office, my little brother hit the vending machine jackpot. I remember that building, with its cement floor, cold and drafty, and how the people who worked there never smiled. I remember the moms standing in long lines, heads usually bowed, while impatient little ones pulled on their legs.

On this particular day, six-year-old Chris had wandered out of line and started messing around with a vending machine, punching the buttons. I went after him, ready to drag him back into line, when suddenly a whole torrent of nickels came clinking out of the change return reservoir. He looked down at the coins, then at me, eyebrows raised and mouth hanging open. His bright blue eyes flashed with excitement, light brown freckles standing out on his fair skin and white-blond hair sticking up as usual.

I could read his mind. *We're rich!* Followed by, *Don't make me take these nickels to the mean-looking lady at the counter!* I glanced at my mom and sisters, still standing in line, and then shot Chris a grin and joined him in stuffing those coins into the pockets of our corduroy pants.

As I look back on that moment, it strikes me as supremely ironic that a vending machine full of candy sat in the middle of a food stamp office filled with people who couldn't afford to buy food for their families.

We carried our cold, silvery treasures home and hid the coins in our jammie drawer. On a Saturday morning a few weeks later, Chris and I got up extra early, while it was still dull and gray outside. Our plan was to sneak out to the candy store four blocks away and across a busy street before our parents got out of bed. Ever the little mommy, I told Chris I had to make him breakfast before we could go.

Neither of us knew what we were doing as we boiled water and plopped in two eggs. I didn't cook them long enough, and when we tried to crack them yellow goo oozed out the sides. I'm pretty sure I made Chris eat that egg anyway before buttoning him into his tan corduroy coat with big brown buttons. I held his hand as we snuck out the garage door and leaned into the cold morning wind. I fretted over his forgetting his hat, but mostly I was thrilled at thinking we were getting away with something.

We made it to the store and back, nickels traded for a brown lunch bag filled with candy. We got caught, of course. Our parents were up and frantic by the time we returned. There were spankings, the candy was confiscated and deposited somewhere in the garage beyond our reach, and there were tears. But it had been a grand kid-adventure, and I wasn't sorry. I couldn't have known, though, that it would be the last adventure I would have with my little brother.

Chris and Marla were twins born just thirteen months after me, although I felt much older. When I was in the third grade, the decision was made to separate Chris and Marla into two different first-grade classes so that Chris could "come into his own." In kindergarten he had been mostly silent, trailing Marla around and allowing her to speak for him.

The day it happened, I saw Chris at recess. He was playing in the sandbox at the back of the school playground, and he waved at me. I didn't wave back but instead turned and ignored him for fear my friends would see me hanging out with the little kids.

After school I went to a friend's house to play, and when I got home it was almost time for *I Love Lucy* at five. I plopped down in front of the television to watch, and it was the episode where Lucy and Ethel worked at a candy factory and messed up the candy on the conveyor belt, trying to fix their mess by shoving candy into their mouths.

I was so absorbed in the show that for once I didn't pay any attention to where my sisters and brother were. Usually I was very attuned to what rooms of the house they were in and what they were doing, just in case my parents started fighting and I had to whisk them away to the basement and distract them with games. But this time Mom was in the kitchen, Dad wasn't home yet, and I was laughing at the antics of Lucy and Ethel. Until my mom started screaming.

It wasn't her normal yelling, and at first I didn't recognize the sound at all. She was on the phone in the kitchen shrieking into the receiver; I tore myself away from my show and ran into the kitchen to see what was happening. I couldn't make sense of it—Chris was laid out on the kitchen table, his fair skin purple.

"I think he's dead," Mom kept saying into the phone.

How can he be dead when his fingers are twitching? That was all I could think.

Then the commotion started. Police. People in the house. Ambulances. Then Mom and Chris disappearing into the back of one, the doors closing with a hollow thump. A neighbor arrived and led my sisters and me into a car and dropped us off at the house of one of Marla's friends from school named Terrie.

Terrie's mom stood in her tiny living room, literally wringing her hands, clearly unsure what to do to comfort or help the three little girls plopped into the middle of her normal afternoon routine.

"I need to be alone with my sisters," I told Terrie's mom. I took my sisters into the backyard, and the three of us huddled together underneath the jungle gym. I knew we needed to pray to the God who lived at Grandma's house. I ordered my sisters to bow their heads.

Marla, who never listened to me, for once did as she was told. Jenny was five and didn't know what was happening but dropped her head with her straight, fine blonde hair falling across her chubby cheeks. It was Good Friday, April 8. I knew that Easter was three days away and that, if we prayed hard enough, God could raise Chris from the dead, just as He had raised Jesus.

My parents came to get us a few hours later. They sat together on the couch in Terrie's living room, unified for once. With pale faces and sad eyes they explained that the doctors had done everything they could. They said that Chris had been playing in the backyard by himself with my jump rope. He had tied the rope to the swing set, forming something like a noose, and had become entangled. My mom had gone to check on him while I was watching Lucy and had found him hanging. He had been without oxygen just long enough that the doctors couldn't make him breathe again.

After midnight the reverend from Holy Cross Lutheran came to our house, sat in the front room, and tried to comfort my parents. I think he prayed, but I was furious at him because he represented God, and God hadn't answered my prayer. The next morning I stood in the backyard under the swing set and screamed at God up in the sky: "I hate you. I will never forgive you!"

I was pretty sure that hating God was an unforgiveable sin, but I was too angry to care because the one person who had always made me feel safe couldn't be trusted after all.

The next few days were a blur with people everywhere in our house and food we couldn't possibly eat piling up on the counters. My parents moved through the house like zombies. Marla was inconsolable at the loss of her soulmate, while Jenny just looked lost. On every surface not covered with casserole dishes stood an Easter lily provided by well-intentioned friends or neighbors. To this day the smell of Easter lilies makes me sick.

For months after my brother's funeral my sisters and I slept in the same bed, and every night I would whisper, "I'm sorry," over and over until I fell asleep. Deep down, I was pretty sure it was my fault that I hadn't kept one of my siblings safe. My parents, briefly united in grief, soon returned to old patterns. If they were broken before my brother's death, they were irreparable afterward.

John and Lisa on their wedding day, 1986

3

What Family Looks Like

Motherhood is an act of infinite optimism.

GILDA RADNER

had just learned I was pregnant. John and I sat outside a clinic in his souped-up, rust-colored 1972 Chevy Nova as the news settled in. We had met while cruising outside the local mall after his muscle car had caught my eye while I was riding around with my friend in her mother's beat-up pea-green Buick.

I wasn't sure why John and his buddies pulled over for us when we motioned to them, but from that very first moment we were inseparable. John made me feel safe. Even at seventeen he was so stable, strong, and kind. We had been dating for one year exactly. He introduced me to his family, and I loved how normal they were. I loved that his parents were married still and that his mom made dinner every night and even how his younger brother and sister bickered at the dinner table. No one yelled at their dinner table. Mostly they laughed and teased one another.

It was February and freezing outside, and John started the car, the huge engine coming to life with a roar and the warm air beginning to flow from the vents. John turned to me and looked straight into my eyes.

"We should get married. What are you doing a week from Friday?"

I laugh now about that teenage marriage proposal. In just ten days our whole world would change. We told my parents first, because I was less scared of their reaction, or maybe I just didn't care as much. I *really* didn't want to tell John's parents, but the next night we were standing in their basement rec room as John's mom did home-dialysis, her blood circulating through a machine that softly whirred next to her recliner. John's dad sat in the armchair next to Michele, watching a movie with her, as they did three times a week.

John and I stood together near the doorway of his basement bedroom. I stared at the gold and brown shag carpet for what seemed like an eternity while John got up the nerve to tell his parents I was pregnant. I was pretty sure the news might kill his mom and couldn't believe we were telling her during dialysis.

"Lisa is pregnant," John finally blurted out.

I'm sure they had suspected this, since we had been standing there frozen for almost an hour, and I expected tears, recrimination, and shame. At first there was just silence. Finally, Michele spoke.

"When are you getting married?"

Although I'm sure she was shocked and saddened that her son's life was not going to go the way she must have dreamed, she didn't sound angry. They spent the next half hour talking to us about marriage and commitment and making clear their expectation that we would care for one another and this baby because we were making a lifelong commitment.

A week later I found a used wedding dress in a thrift shop, and John's mom had planned a small wedding with pretty purple flowers and a little reception back at their home. A few family members from out of town on both our sides were going to fly in on short notice.

I still remember feeling surprised and validated when John's grandma and great aunt and my great uncle decided to make the quick trip to attend the little ceremony at Holy Cross Lutheran Church, the very church I had attended as a child, where a large plum tree grew in the yard, planted as a memorial for my brother, Chris. Somehow the presence of out-of-town family felt like a sign that this was a real marriage, a real wedding.

Then the night before our wedding the most remarkable thing happened—at the worst possible time. John's mom received the call that a perfect kidney donor match had come in. Michele would need to be at the hospital within the hour if she wanted to receive this life-changing, life-affording gift. The timing was an awful blow for John. He wanted to postpone the wedding so his mom wouldn't miss it, but she wouldn't hear of it. Family had come into town, we were going to go forward . . . and that was that.

We drove to the hospital together:

Me.

John.

His sister Wendy, who was just one year older and had often shouldered the responsibility of helping with the family when her mom was ill.

Thirteen-year-old Scott, the ever jokester, now pale and quiet.

And Shelley, the littlest, who wasn't quite sure what was happening but was happy she would still get to wear her pretty new purple dress for the wedding the next day.

We all waited in that overly bright hospital waiting room until one o'clock in the morning, hardly stirring from the uncomfortable orange plastic chairs for hours, until the surgeon finally came in to talk to John's dad and to give us the news that the surgery had been a success and that Michele was doing well. John's dad became emotional, a rarity for him, and John and his brother and sisters crowded around their dad with relief and joy.

Just eight hours later we were all at the church, minus the most important woman in the Steven family's lives. John was dressed in the new suit his mom had bought him, his brown hair feathered back and the mullet trimmed so it just reached his starched white collar. I squeezed into the slightly-too-tight wedding dress and fought back the morning sickness, praying that I wouldn't get sick before the vows.

Because we had booked the church so rapidly, there had been no way to reschedule the renovation work that had begun in the sanctuary. As John's grandma struck up the wedding march on the old organ at the front of the church, I walked down an aisle flanked by construction scaffolding. The workmen hadn't even been called off for the day; they just quietly went to the back of the church and sat and watched our little ceremony. I barely remember our vows, but I do remember John looking me straight in the eye and truly meaning it when he said, "I do."

When I look back on grainy photos from that day, I'm smiling with my lips tightly closed. I didn't want anyone to see my braces. John's uncle filmed the wedding so Michele could watch it. The little gathering at John's house after the ceremony went just as Michele had planned, and we felt celebrated, even while missing her greatly.

Ten years later we would renew our vows in our own church, with our three kids by our side and John's mom crying in the front row. We did it for her as much as for a recommitment of our marriage. After all, she was the one who had taught us what family is supposed to look like.

My own family had come apart at the seams years earlier. After my brother died we had moved to Wyoming, where my dad got a job on an oil rig. We lived in a trailer park on the outskirts of a town so small that the post office and grocery store were housed in the same building. The elementary, middle, and high school were the biggest buildings in town because kids from surrounding rural areas were bussed into Lyman to go to school.

My parents' fights had intensified in proportion to my dad's drinking. I often hid my sisters in the closet of the bedroom and played Strawberry Shortcake with them to distract them from the yelling and slamming doors. Moving to Wyoming had only served to isolate my mom from any support she'd once had, and at the age of thirteen I was her main confidante and support.

When my mom took a job as the elementary school secretary, my dad lost it. He became more and more irrational, often accusing my mom of cheating on him with someone at the school. One night I was helping my mom make dinner in our tiny kitchen. I was peeling potatoes when I heard my dad's car crunching over the dirt drive next to the trailer. I couldn't figure out why it was taking him so long to come into the house, but I finally heard the back door that led into the laundry room creak open.

My mom and I both turned, and I saw that my dad had my grandpa's rifle in his arms, wrapped in a blue and gold towel. He didn't say a word, just walked into the bedroom and started bumping around in the closet. My mom's eyes had gone wide with alarm, but she didn't speak, just carried on making hamburger patties.

That night my dad chased my mom around the trailer, shouting at her to swear on the Bible that she wasn't cheating. She finally locked herself in the bathroom across the hall from my little bedroom. When my dad broke down the bathroom door with a great crash, I dove under my bed, hiding there for the rest of the night.

The next morning, as soon as my dad left for work, my mom started throwing clothes and personal items into an old, scarred gray suitcase. She was frantic and told me to pack my backpack quickly and help my sisters do the same. I raced to my room, matching her sense of urgency, and began stuffing clothes into my school backpack.

I was pretty sure we were never going to return to that battered little trailer, and I didn't know if I would ever see my things again. My school backpack didn't hold much, but I shoved in the blue bunny I still slept with, along with the little pair of orange and green pajamas I kept in the bottom of my drawer that had belonged to Chris.

I emerged from my room to find Marla and my mom in a showdown. My mom was shouting about leaving for our grandparents' house.

"We have to catch a bus to Denver. There's no time to waste!"

I ended up having to physically haul my sister into the backseat of our broken-down old Jeep. I climbed into the front seat, trying not to throw up. We drove to the elementary school first, and my mom asked me to run in and let the other secretary know that she wouldn't be in that day.

All the lights inside the school felt too bright as I approached the front desk. I was mortified when the principal of the school wandered out of his office, a friendly smile on his face, joking with me that I must be playing hooky from the middle school next door.

He must have known something was pretty wrong, though, once he saw my face. His smile faltered as I mumbled that my mom was sick and couldn't come to work—and then quickly turned and fled out the front door. *We have to make that bus.* If we didn't, I was sure we would end up being one of those headlines in the morning newspaper.

⚷

What most people don't recognize about teen moms is their grit. They have determination, they are problem solvers, they are flexible, and they are unselfish caregivers. It's an indefinable grit you can't teach. It comes because teen moms start the hard stuff of life much earlier than the average kid. They don't have the luxury of going straight from high school to college and then graduating, getting a job, and slowly growing into the responsibilities of adulthood.

Teen moms are often caregivers for other family members in multigenerational households. They care deeply for their families, even if they've been hurt or neglected by family members with mental illness, addiction, or other issues. They weather negative messages about themselves, judgment from people in general, and stereotypes and statistics that tell them they're a failure before they've even had a chance to try.

They're not very trusting, and it's hard for them to be vulnerable or ask for help, so it's critical that the first things they experience when they walk through the doors of our Hope House Resource Center are a warm welcome, a big hug, and a genuine interest in their adorable little ones.

Marisa wasn't one for those big hugs. She had such a chip on her shoulder when she first came to Hope House. She was seventeen, with a one-year-old baby girl, and she needed her GED. She would show up for class, but always with an attitude. I had worked with intimidating girls before, but Marisa was on a different level.

She was a little thing, probably 5'3", but the way she stood—back straight, big brown eyes flashing with defiance—made her seem bigger. Unlike some of the girls who came heavily laden with shame, Marisa would look you straight in the eye, unflinching. She was tough for a reason.

Marisa had been just eleven years old when her big brother had gotten her involved with his gang. Girls who enter gangs are often used horribly, and it can be a matter of safety to have a boyfriend to protect you from other male gang members. Marisa was fourteen when she began dating TJ. He made promises, said he would take care of her, and pledged to teach her the "family business."

He taught Marisa that the trade secret was to never taste the product you sell. Unfortunately, he didn't follow his own rule for long, and soon TJ became the gang member she was most afraid of. He wouldn't hesitate to use violence to intimidate her.

When she got pregnant at sixteen, things got better for a bit. Her baby girl was the most beautiful little thing, and Marisa would cradle her and sing her Mexican lullabies to cover the sounds of partying in the home where she lived with TJ and several others. She wanted a way out for her little girl, and she knew the first step was to get her GED.

Unfortunately, Marisa was still so young and so hotheaded that she didn't last long in the Hope House GED Program. She just quietly disappeared one day, and even though she had been challenging, I missed her. Whenever one of our moms left Hope House, it felt a little like a personal failure. I would often question whether I had done enough or said the right things, or if I had pushed too hard for progress.

Working with our teen moms means putting your heart on the line every day. The only way to truly make change in their lives is to invest in them far beyond teaching, coaching, or assisting with resources. Our staff members truly *love* our teen moms, with a fierce, protective mama-bear love.

This is something our girls have seldom experienced before, and it opens their hearts to change. It also opens our own hearts to deep sadness and worry. For weeks after Marisa disappeared, I would lie in bed at night and wonder what was happening to her and to little Neesy. This was in the early days at Hope House, but I knew enough by then to realize that Marisa had returned to a violent and scary existence.

Two years later Marisa came back to Hope House, toting Neesy and visibly pregnant with her second baby. My heart leapt when I saw her coming through the door, and my first instinct was to run to her, hug her, and barrage her with questions. But the guarded look in her eye told me to wait, to give her time. I settled for a quick hug and a warm welcome back, but inside I was flooded with a deep relief to see this girl alive.

There was something tangibly different about Marisa after her return to Hope House. She was nineteen years old then, and her determination to change her life was clear. She showed up every day, enduring a long bus ride with an energetic toddler, and worked hard in the GED class.

I was shocked when she agreed to be matched with a mentor, a sign that she was ready to explore new relationships in her life. Julie was the perfect mentor for Marisa, having grown up in difficult circumstances herself. Julie, along with our staff, poured love and grace into Marisa's life whenever she would allow it.

Marisa had always had to care for herself, her younger siblings, and her mom. For the first time in her life someone was there to take care of *her*. As Marisa's relationship and level of trust with Julie deepened, she began sharing bits and pieces of her life from the past two years.

Her now ex-boyfriend, TJ, had been involved in a drive-by shooting that had left TJ wounded and his best friend dead. Marisa knew at that point that something had to change. She was terrified by the very real danger she and Neesy were in. She moved back in with her mom and made the decision to return to Hope House, now willing to accept the structure and expectations she knew were a part of our program. But more importantly, in a show of grit, Marisa was willing to open herself up to healthy relationships.

Vanessa with her son, Aayden, 2012

4

Second Chances

If you are still breathing, you have a second chance.

OPRAH WINFREY

Vanessa had a smile that made you feel that she liked you from the first moment she met you. That smile lit up her whole face and made it all the way to her eyes, which was pretty surprising, considering all she'd been through. Aayden was only a toddler, but he already had his mama's smile when they moved into Hope House. That boy would light up with surprise every time he saw or heard something new. His bushy little eyebrows would shoot up, and his lips would form a perfect O. His mom may have been only fifteen when she'd had him, but this little boy knew he was loved.

Vanessa wasn't shy or guarded when she and Aayden first arrived. She wasn't angry, watchful, or reserved, as so many teen moms were when they moved into the house. She laughed all the time, and everyone liked her immediately. She loved our Residential Manager, Nicole, who had a similar sense of fun and often initiated games with the girls.

I still laugh when I think about that hot July day, as I was trying to work in my little office with a barely adequate window cooler blowing on my face. I was trying to concentrate when laughter and shrieks erupted outside my window. Glancing out at the wide green yard, I saw that Vanessa had initiated a water balloon fight and that Nicole was out there chasing the girls up and down the yard, right in the thick of it.

What the heck? I thought. My office was stifling, and I couldn't think anyway, so I strolled outside to watch the fun. It was one of those moments God gives you when you just feel lucky to be a part of something. Those girls, whose lives had been so full of pain and whose responsibilities were so heavy, were just being kids with their own kids and their staff. They were making the kind of memory they wanted for their children.

I reached down to the big bucket of water balloons on the deck and grabbed a pink one, cold and sloshy. I hid it behind my back and walked down the steps to the yard; then, right when Vanessa looked over at me, I tossed it at her arm and the balloon broke, sending a small river of cold water down her shoulder and back. Her eyebrows shot up, and her mouth made the exact same surprised *O* that Aayden's always did.

I should have known I was in trouble. It took about two seconds for her to pull back her arm and take aim, and before I knew it she was chasing me through the church parking lot next door, determined to peg me—which didn't take long, since she was fast and athletic, and I was in heels and a skirt. It was one of those golden days, one you hold onto when the gray days come.

By October it was pretty clear that Vanessa was chasing something, trying to fill a void by making her dream of a perfect family a reality. She had reconnected with her high school boyfriend—not Aayden's dad but a young man she related to because he also had a hard story and was so nice to Aayden.

Just like a real father would be, she must have thought. But she couldn't *really* know, never having met her own father. Her childhood had been filled with abuse by the man her mother had married when Vanessa was five, and then by the step-grandfather who had moved in with them when she was twelve.

True to form, Vanessa didn't sneak around; she just openly shared with the staff that she and Brian were going to move to Texas to live with Brian's mom. She had so willingly placed her trust in the hands of her surrogate "aunties" at Hope House that it had never even occurred to her that we would be anything but happy for her.

That's the thing about working with our girls. They aren't court ordered to stay with us or participate in our programs. They are young and hurt, and it really is true that their brains aren't fully developed. Just as with any teenager, they can't see as far into the future as the adults in their lives can.

Melinda, our Parenting Educator for many years, often joked with the girls about whether their latest grand idea or overreaction to a situation might be "thinking with their lizard brain." We serve our girls until they turn twenty-five years old, and they can always come back after leaving our programs, just as long as they come back ready to work hard. It always amazes the younger staff how often a mom returns at age twenty or twenty-one, sometimes not having spoken to anyone at Hope House for two years or longer.

Our staff never gives up, texting and messaging encouragement for as long as we have contact information for a mom. We understand that, if they aren't communicating with us, it's often because they feel ashamed of what is going on in their lives and don't want us to know. They don't want to let us down. Sometimes their lives have caved in again, and they're so busy navigating one crisis after another that they can't focus on their own journeys to self-sufficiency.

So often it's a Halloween party or a Santa's workshop that will allow a mom the opportunity to reconnect. Her head is usually hung low, afraid of the judgment she thinks she deserves for poor decisions made a year or longer before. The look on a teen mom's face when she walks in and hears a chorus of happy staff members calling her name and rushing over for hugs—it's a look almost of shock, followed by wonder. It never ceases to amaze me that they are so surprised to be welcomed back, to realize that they were truly missed and that home was right there waiting all along.

So, when Vanessa left Hope House with a happy wave and a two-year-old boy balanced on her hip, I felt a wave of sadness, knowing that she would almost certainly be walking into more pain with this sudden choice. However, I also had a kernel of hope. Vanessa knew the way home if she ever wanted to come back.

God can make something beautiful from something broken—I have always believed this . . . or so I thought. In reality it took me a long time to realize that I mostly believed it to be true for others. Not for me. Every day I watched as God stitched together something beautiful through the broken lives of our teen moms—girls like Vanessa, who, just like Alondra, would one day stand on a stage before five hundred people at our annual gala and bravely tell her story. And yes, Vanessa's story did indeed become more painful before she returned to us, finally ready to let God mend her and heal others through her brave example.

Vanessa didn't just share at that gala that she had been a teen mom—she shared about the sexual abuse; the deep betrayal of a mom who wouldn't believe her; and the attempts to find something, anything, to fill the gaping holes. She shared about coming to Hope House the first time, covering up her emptiness with a bright smile, and her confusion at finding a place so warm, accepting, and loving that it couldn't be real.

Then she talked about coming back to Hope House three years later, desperate, embarrassed, back with her mom, and desperately seeking a way forward in life. In her speech Vanessa shared what it had been like to return to the only safe place she had ever known, filled with shame but stunned to find that the people there had never given up on her. In that moment she believed what we had been telling her all along: that God loved her, that nothing that had happened to her and nothing she had done could ever stop our God from loving her and having a plan for her life.

I was so proud of that girl as she stood tall on the stage, beautiful in her bright red gown, which swept the floor above her too-high heels, her dark curls tumbling down her shoulders. I knew how nervous she was, but it didn't show. So poised and confident at twenty-one years old. I had taken the stage shortly before her and had talked about having been a teen mom myself, married at seventeen, and about my heart for teen moms and for giving them a second chance.

I have never had trouble sharing about my having become a mom so early and about how God had used that openness to fuel my passion for giving teen moms a second chance. What I wouldn't share was how I had become a teen mom in the first place. The truth was that, while I related to being a teen mom and had experienced the same judgment and disregard as our girls, I actually connected with them at a much deeper level.

I knew the *fear* they felt—the fear of repeating the patterns we had grown up with and the fear of doing it wrong, because no one had ever shown us what parenting was supposed to look like.

Marisa with her children, 2014

5

A Chance to Be a Leader

"You gain strength, courage and
confidence by every experience
in which you really stop to look fear in the face.
You must do the thing you think you cannot do."

ELEANOR ROOSEVELT

The day Marisa walked across the GED stage in her cap and gown, flashing me her incredibly beautiful smile before throwing her arms around me, was one of the sweetest moments of my life. How was it possible that God had entrusted *me* with this precious little piece of His kingdom—this bold, brave, extraordinary girl who was no longer lost but had a place to belong?

I had a dream to help teen moms, but at every step along the way I knew I was just a former teen mom myself, with no college degree, no formal training, and no career experience. In my heart of hearts I was often still a scared, lonely kid whose chaotic childhood had been marked by situational poverty, tragic loss, and the same gut-level fear of violent outbursts that Marisa had experienced.

Still, beginning at seventeen I'd had something that Marisa, who was shackled by the chains of generational poverty, had never experienced. Even though my home had been broken, I had grown up surrounded by middle-class family members, and when I became pregnant I was welcomed into John's loving family, who showed me how structure, stability, and faith could anchor my own soon-to-be little family.

In fact, when my son, Johnny, was just six-months old, my mother-in-law, Michele, decided that I should have a baby shower, just as any other new mom would. Because I didn't have any friends to invite, she hosted it at her house and invited all of her friends, known as the Fenton Street Gang because they had all met while living on that street. Those women didn't know me, but they came to celebrate me and my little boy because Michele accepted me and loved me, which meant that they would, too.

In time my new mother-in-law would become an inspiration for my own leadership journey. Michele was a beautiful woman, small in stature with soft brown curls and big brown eyes. She was quick to laugh, quick to tease her kids in a loving way, and smart as a whip in running the family business with my father-in-law, John.

Michele had every excuse to have raised a broken family herself. She and my father-in-law had fought for their marriage, their business, and their family since my husband, John, was just a little boy and Michele had been diagnosed with kidney failure after strep throat had attacked her kidneys during her fourth pregnancy. She had undergone regular dialysis at home for John's entire childhood, and besides her family there were two things that had gotten her through: her friends at MOPS and her faith.

Michele was diagnosed in 1974, just a few short months after her neighborhood friends on Fenton Street had started a little group they called MOPS, or Mothers of Preschoolers. There were eight women, and they met around a little table in a Sunday school room at Trinity Baptist Church in Wheat Ridge, Colorado, five minutes from their homes on Fenton Street. They hired a sitter to watch the kids while they shared a snack, made a craft, and had two whole child-free hours in which to finish a sentence without interruption.

After having grown up in an old-fashioned Catholic environment where nuns cracked the hands of children with rulers, Michele was not a fan of religion. She had met her husband, John, when they were in Catholic School together growing up in Crystal Lake, Illinois. She told stories about the nuns and how they scared the children into good behavior. She and the other kids had once been told that it would be a mortal sin if they were to step on the new grass that had been planted in the churchyard.

But somehow these new friends of hers seemed different when they talked about their God. It almost seemed as if they *knew* Him. In fact, they often brought their Bibles along to MOPS, and they all seemed to know the words inside, which was surprising to Michele, as only priests and nuns had carried Bibles when she was a kid.

Word began to get out about this little group of women. Soon the first ever MOPS group began to grow, with more moms showing up each month. It turned out that this little group from Fenton Street was onto something. Moms were in desperate need of connection with one another and with God.

When Michele became ill, her MOPS group surrounded her, making meals for her family, caring for her children when she had to go to the hospital, and praying for her recovery. My mother-in-law became a believer because her MOPS friends demonstrated the love of Christ to her during her darkest days. Years later, though I am sure her heart broke over lost dreams for her son, this woman would welcome me into her family, love me as Christ did, and encourage me to find other moms to connect with by going to MOPS myself.

By 1986, when I got married and became a mom at seventeen, MOPS had incorporated as a nonprofit and grown into an international ministry, with MOPS groups in every single state and seven other countries. MOPS was now led by CEO Elisa Morgan, an incredible Christian author, speaker, and leader.

Meanwhile, I was nineteen years old and had a two-year-old son, a struggling marriage, and no friends. My mother-in-law knew I needed connection, but in my mind all those moms in MOPS groups across the country were the ones who had "done it right." There was no way I belonged, or that they would accept me—a teenage mom who had finished high school by correspondence course. I would go, but only because I loved my mother-in-law and wanted her to be proud of me.

As I drove into the church parking lot on that first day of MOPS, my heart pounded so hard it hurt. I was literally shaking in my black faux leather boots. I unstrapped Johnny from his car seat and hoisted him onto my hip. At two-years-old he was already a big boy, weighing more than most kids his age, and independent.

Even as a toddler he wasn't one for snuggles, and he immediately began to wiggle and demand to get down. I clutched him more tightly. There was no way I was letting him down in the parking lot and risking his pulling his chubby little fist out of mine, as he was prone to do. These ladies probably already thought I was a bad mom, and I wasn't going to confirm it by having to chase my independent toddler through the parking lot.

I was surprised when the woman at the door met me with a wide, welcoming smile and introduced herself as Julie Schroeder. Her blonde hair was pulled back in a ponytail, and her deep brown eyes were warm and friendly as she pointed me toward the children's rooms. Johnny was ecstatic to get out of my tight grip and ran straight into the two-year-old room, excited to play with all the new toys and the other toddlers.

Without my little human shield, I had to take a deep breath and enter the big room full of other women, all of whom seemed so much more put together than I felt. Yet every single mom that morning gave me a warm smile and a word of encouragement. It seemed as if they actually *liked* me!

I soon began living for those MOPS meetings, unable to contain my excitement at having found a place where I could connect with other moms. My son was the center of my world, but I didn't know anything about being a good mom. I absorbed everything I could from our group speakers, our discussion time, and the more experienced moms around me.

My mother-in-law had given me a Bible, and I found myself opening it up occasionally, just to look up some biblical parenting principle that the other MOPS moms were talking about. I even started taking Johnny to church by myself, as John wasn't interested. He hadn't been inside a church since we had visited a neighborhood pastor about baptizing Johnny when he was six months old.

That pastor had gone from welcoming and smiling to literally counting on his fingers after asking when we had gotten married and how old Johnny was. As soon as he made the connection that we had been teen parents and pregnant before we married, he became cold and rude. John said that he didn't need the judgment, and after the baptism we never went back.

But the moms at MOPS were different. They prayed for one another and even prayed out loud—something I had never heard in the little Lutheran church I had grown up in, which had always been a refuge of orderliness but had never taught me about this "personal relationship with Jesus" that my MOPS friends talked about. I felt as if I knew who Jesus was—there had certainly been times as a child when I'd had no one else to rely on—but I had never known you could *grow* in your relationship with Him.

Increasingly curious, I would ask Michele questions. She encouraged me to try to have a few quiet moments to myself in the morning before Johnny woke up to pray and to use that time to ask God my questions and then to read the Bible for a few minutes. She told me how surprised she had been years earlier to feel God quietly speaking to her through the words in His book. Reading the Bible is a practice I have incorporated into my life ever since, and although God doesn't speak out loud, and it sometimes feels as if I'm reading the Word by rote habit, it has been the single greatest way in which I have come to know Jesus better.

I'll never forget the morning our MOPS Leader, Lynn Chapman, approached me as I was packing up Johnny after MOPS. Lynn was one of those women who made you feel instantly at ease. She never seemed nervous when she was at the microphone speaking to the whole MOPS group. With four rambunctious kids under the age of eight, she somehow seemed to have an endless reserve of patience. I admired and looked up to this woman, and I couldn't believe it when she asked me a question: "Lisa, would you consider volunteering to co-lead the Moppets Program?"

I'm sure I stared at her in shock.

"With Julia Schroeder. Next fall," she added.

Does she know I am only twenty years old? Although I was surprised, my heart leapt at the invitation partly because I loved little kids—and partly because I was flattered to be noticed. I hadn't yet learned the wisdom of praying for guidance from God before accepting an invitation to join Him in His work, so I immediately and excitedly agreed.

That night, after reading Johnny his favorite board book three times and getting him down to sleep, I had time to reflect on how I really felt. I had never been asked to help lead anything before, and it wasn't just that I felt honored, although I certainly did. It was that someone actually thought I had *value.* I was a bit older now, but I still felt like a teen mom, someone with no voice and no power.

I didn't feel all that far beyond that eighteen-year-old girl I had been, taking my six-month-old in for shots at the local clinic, only to be judged by a cold, stern doctor who hadn't liked me from the moment she laid eyes on me. She had been short and rude during the visit, clearly judging me as unfit, based simply on my age.

Just a few days later there was a knock on my door in the middle of the day, while Johnny was napping, and a social worker from Child Protective Services stood on the front step. The doctor had reported that Johnny had deep scratches on his back, which had been a total lie. The woman was kind enough but quite firm that she had to look at Johnny and make sure he was okay.

My mind was racing as I went to lift Johnny from his crib. *What if he is crabby because I woke him up? If he cries a lot, she might think something is wrong with him.* I was terrified as I placed my chubby baby boy into that woman's arms, warm from sleep and thankfully all smiles and coos for his new friend. Johnny did his best to charm the social worker, batting his huge blue eyes like a pro while she gently lifted his shirt and examined his skin.

After the woman had placed Johnny back in my arms, reassuring me that everything looked fine, she let herself out the front door. My legs immediately turned to jelly, and I placed Johnny in his playpen and started bawling. It may not have been true, but in my eighteen-year-old mind that woman could have simply walked into my home and walked out with my son. If there had been anything out of place, anything she had thought was wrong, I told myself, I could have lost him. This was one of my most powerless moments as a teen mother.

Knowing that Lynn saw something in me, something that made me seem worthy to be a leader, went much deeper than that first sense of feeling flattered. Her invitation meant that someone actually thought I had something to offer, something to give to others.

By this time in our new family I was doing home daycare to help pay family bills, and John was working for his dad at the family machine shop. I would wait until Johnny and the other children were down for a nap and then work frantically on a new curriculum for Moppets that I was developing, with stories and Bible crafts for the kids. I absolutely loved it. I loved being trusted to make a difference, and I loved those leadership meetings where I got to be included in decision making for the MOPS group. I became more confident in sharing my opinion.

My co-leader was a woman in her sixties who had raised three children and had a handful of grandchildren. She loved the kids, but she had a hard time keeping our volunteer Moppets teachers engaged. I began to see ways in which I could solve this problem, from improving our teacher training to having more direct communication with teachers. Before long I found myself going around my co-leader and making phone calls to volunteers without telling her, even giving direction and instruction without including her in the discussion.

Then came the day, as I was busily putting away craft material, that our pastor's wife, Sandy, who served as the lead teacher of our MOPS group, pulled me aside. "Can we talk privately?" she asked. I had great respect for Sandy. She had survived a battle with cancer, and I had also watched her in awe during our leadership team meetings, amazed at her depth of faith and desire to continue to give to the young mothers in our church even as she fought the hardest battle of her life. It hit me all the harder, therefore, when she gently but firmly let me know that it had come to her attention that I had been making decisions about the Moppets Program without including my co-leader.

I was defensive at first and tried to share how much more efficient we had become, and how fewer volunteer absences there were. She just shook her head at me and softly said, "That isn't the point. We are a leadership *team*; you have been acting on your own."

My stomach began to hurt as Sandy continued to explain, and I realized she was right. I might have had youthful exuberance, but my co-leader had years of experience, and my actions had been disrespectful of her.

I knew I needed to call my co-leader and apologize, but I was truly embarrassed; if I were honest with myself, I was also a bit scared. I had grown up with a father who seldom took responsibility for his actions or the hurt he caused others, and he wasn't the forgiving type when you made a mistake yourself. Apologizing didn't get you off the hook with him. What if my co-leader was really mad; had hurt feelings; or worst of all, told me she didn't think I could be her co-leader anymore?

When I made the call later that day my hand shook so badly that I could barely hold the phone. I took a big breath, threw God a silent prayer for the right words, and then closed my eyes tightly when my co-leader picked up. I dove right in and apologized for my actions and for getting ahead of her—and also getting ahead of God. As the true leader she was, she shared how my actions had affected her and then graciously offered her forgiveness and even her support of my new ideas. She had just wanted to be included in them. By the time I got off the phone I felt a ton better, but I had also learned a couple of important lessons.

Being in charge of something does not equal being a leader. I would need to get better at seeking God's direction before acting, and I would need to be willing to follow those whom God had clearly placed in front of me as leaders. Sandy, my sweet, wise teaching leader, also taught me that *leadership isn't about me.* It's about *Him,* and about the little piece of His kingdom that He has entrusted to my care. In my haste to make improvements, I hadn't really been thinking about the Moppets Program as I claimed to have been but had been trying to prove my own value and worth to my older and wiser leaders.

Looking back, I can see now that those lessons, although I was bound to repeat some mistakes, were the first few steps in a leadership journey that would one day allow me to stand on that stage with Marisa.

6

The Great Smackdown

"Be still, and know that I am God."

PSALM 46:10

I juggled a plate full of freshly baked Valentine's Day cookies, sweet little hearts with bright pink frosting, as I climbed out of my car. Whenever there was a new girl, we liked to welcome her to MOPS with a plate of homemade cookies. Liz was the new girl, a seventeen-year-old teen mom, and I had arrived on a mission to deliver the cookies and then drive her to a Teen MOPS meeting at our church.

The narrow front walk was cracked, the tiny yard was dusty and devoid of grass, and several empty brown beer bottles peeped from underneath a straggly frozen bush near the front door. Feeling a little nervous, I gripped the plate of cookies in one hand and knocked on the freezing aluminum door with the other. I stepped back involuntarily as the door squeaked open and a clearly inebriated man stood swaying in the doorway. The skin beneath his bristly beard was yellow, and he had huge bags underneath his eyes.

Is he drunk? What have I gotten myself into?

I took a deep breath. "I'm here for Liz," I stammered, holding out the plate of cookies. Taking the plate from my hand, the man turned and hollered into the gloomy recesses of the house.

"Liz! Your friend is here!" he shouted as he disappeared into the shadowy living room.

I could make out two small children glued to a television screen and an adult who seemed to be passed out on the couch. I waited nervously for a minute or two before a thin blonde girl appeared and, pushing past me, quickly closed the door to the little red brick home. She started talking nervously, thanking me for coming and bouncing an adorable nine-month-old baby girl on her hip.

On the short drive to the church where our Teen MOPS group met, I learned more about Liz's story. Like many of the girls in our group, Liz was trying to juggle school, parenthood, and a terribly unstable home life. She felt lonely and isolated, and when she'd heard about Teen MOPS while on a visit with baby Madison to the local clinic, she was just desperate enough to push past her natural shyness and reach out. She was so excited to connect with other young moms and maybe even make a friend. Not so different from every other MOPS mom who craved relationship with mom-friends.

It was 1997 and just the year before MOPS International had created a new ministry to serve teen moms, calling it Teen MOPS. When our MOPS group at Arvada Covenant Church decided to launch a Teen MOPS group, I jumped at the chance to co-create the group with a woman named Terrie Kearney. My own days as a MOPS mom were coming to a close by this time. John and I had added two more children to our family, Nate and Heather, and our daughter was just entering kindergarten.

John and his dad ran a busy machine shop, and John had started coming to church with us after having attended a large men's rally. Our life was full of church and parent-teacher conferences and flag football games, but the thought of starting a MOPS group just for teen moms made my heart beat faster. MOPS had literally changed my life, offering me a place to form friendships, learn to be a mom, and even learn to lead.

The Teen MOPS group at Arvada Covenant would be just the second group to form in the whole country, and we weren't given much to work with. Our leadership team for MOPS had detailed handbooks, position descriptions, and templates for running meetings. For Teen MOPS, we had just four pages of basic instructions stapled together at the corner. Starting our little Teen MOPS group was going to involve trial by fire. I remember spending hours in Terrie's living room talking through where to meet (*Will teen moms be intimidated to meet in a church?*); how to even find teen moms (*Can we just put up notices at the WIC office?*); and whether the traditional MOPS meeting model would work (*Do teen moms even want to do crafts?*).

In the end we found that teen moms are no different from any other moms in some regards. They desperately want to be good moms and need relationship with other moms. It wasn't long before we had a fledgling group of teen moms meeting regularly, and we soaked up all that we could learn from them. We found out how important it is to provide transportation, and we learned that food stamps can buy only food, so we started a little MOPS Shop to provide cleaning supplies, paper goods, and diapers.

When a sweet little mama named Kate told us that she loved brownies, we made homemade brownies for the next meeting. Kate literally cried. She said that no one had ever made her homemade brownies before. Simple acts of kindness helped build trust, and soon our teen moms were sharing stories of their lives with us.

I remember being shocked when one mom told me that she and her baby had hidden in the mall when they locked down for the night because she didn't have any other place to sleep. Another mom, nine months pregnant with her second baby, told me how her boyfriend had wanted her to lie on top of the drug money when a rival gang member had busted into their apartment, because he didn't think they would make a pregnant girl move off the couch.

As for Liz, it turned out that her stepfather was as ill as he had looked; he died of alcohol poisoning several months after Liz had joined our Teen MOPS group. After his death, Liz and her mom and little Madison moved into a nearby apartment complex. Liz's mother also struggled with alcohol and couldn't keep a job. The day Liz turned eighteen her mother moved out, leaving Liz alone and taking an apartment three doors down. It was a one-bedroom and more affordable, she said. I was horrified at this abandonment, but Liz brushed it off, telling me that she was better off on her own anyway.

Still in high school and with a minimum wage job at Subway, it wasn't long before Liz and Madison were evicted. Homeless and desperate, Liz moved in with an older woman she had met at her job. The woman's son lived in the basement of the house with a separate entrance, so Liz rarely saw him. She had no idea he was running a methamphetamine lab until she was awakened in the middle of the night by a police raid. Everyone in the house was arrested, and Liz was put in handcuffs, looking on as her daughter was placed in the arms of a social worker.

Visiting Liz in the county jail was another in a string of first experiences for me with our teen moms. It was just like on TV, with thick glass between me and Liz and a grimy phone I had to pick up to talk with her. Except this wasn't TV. The face on the other side of that glass was one of *my* girls.

Dressed in an orange jumpsuit, with curly blonde hair pulled up in a ponytail and a face scrubbed of makeup, Liz looked closer to twelve than eighteen. How was it possible that this sweet girl, who just wanted to be a good mama to her baby, had ended up in jail? Her own mom had left her, she was just a kid herself, and she had done the best she could to keep a roof over Madison's head.

There hadn't been anywhere safe for her to go. The unfairness of it all broke my heart—Liz had been incarcerated for circumstances completely beyond her control, and I saw and felt her confusion. *How did this happen?* she must have been wondering. She didn't even seem angry, really. Just confused and lost. It was heartbreaking, and while my adrenaline shot up as I tried to figure out how to help her, there was nothing I could do in the moment. I cried and prayed on the way home.

It turned out that we weren't alone in our struggle to figure out how to support our teen moms. As more Teen MOPS groups began to pop up around the country, Terrie and I started getting calls from other leaders whose girls were experiencing similar stories of hurt, betrayal, and loss. Everyone was desperate for more guidance on how to run a Teen MOPS group. Even though we had been running our group for only a year, we had more experience than most. After a lot of discussion, Terrie and I, along with our co-leader, Karen Rensink, volunteered to write a handbook for MOPS International specific to Teen MOPS.

The three of us flung ourselves into the research and writing, meeting weekly in Terrie's spare bedroom and covering the walls with sticky notes while filling the trashcan with crumpled rough drafts. It would take a full year and over five hundred hours to complete that handbook, and I felt as if I were eating and breathing Teen MOPS on a daily basis. The truth was, though, that I really enjoyed the feeling of being an "expert" in something.

My head swelled further when my co-authors and I were asked to lead a workshop at the next national MOPS convention. I felt so important, so *successful*. I was going to fly to Chicago to share my knowledge and experience with people who actually thought I had something to say.

I bought a brand-new suit and felt so professional—until we arrived at our workshop, only to find that we had been set up in a hallway. MOPS hadn't even given us a conference room! Still, our little workshop was so full that more chairs had to be brought in. *Wow, we're kind of a big deal,* I thought. I never even noticed that this was becoming more about *me* than it was about teen moms or Teen MOPS.

I was so excited about connecting with other group leaders at the convention and afterward had so many ideas about how Teen MOPS groups could be better supported. I began inviting myself to meetings and pestering leadership at the national level. Looking back, I remember one particularly cringe-worthy call I made to Elisa Morgan, the CEO of MOPS International. How on earth I'd even had her phone number is a mystery.

At that time Elisa Morgan was already an acclaimed author and speaker. She had been named by *Christianity Today* as one of the top fifty women influencing church and culture. But me? I was just a volunteer in a local Teen MOPS group, but somehow I was sure that what I had to say was important enough to personally call the CEO of MOPS and ask for a meeting with her and a few key board members so I could set them straight on how to run Teen MOPS.

I'm pretty sure God just shakes His head at me sometimes.

Surprisingly, Elisa was gracious enough to schedule a meeting with me. I meticulously prepared for that meeting and showed up at the MOPS International offices on a sunny June day in Denver with facts and figures and program details. I was confident and full of passion as I settled into an adjustable chair in the little conference room across from Elisa, who looked stunning and professional with her short, cropped hair and crisp button-down blouse. Two board members joined us, both in suits. I didn't even have the humility to feel intimidated, but I should have.

Normally I'm pretty articulate. I can be persuasive, maybe even inspiring. This had started when I was young—I would turn around and see others following me, like the pied piper of small kids. As I got older I learned how to use encouragement and a sincere tone to influence others. I could aways get a smile from my grandmother by complimenting her cooking or telling her she smelled like chocolate. In high school, drama class had helped me hone my presentation skills, and now in MOPS I was really good at roping in volunteers and convincing them to help. This was going to be a piece of cake.

But from the moment Elisa turned to me and asked me to share what was on my mind, I could barely speak a word. *What is wrong with me?* All of my carefully constructed arguments about MOPS needing to hire more staff and put more focus on Teen MOPS just fled my mind. I couldn't form a coherent sentence!

I *knew* I was right, so how come everyone else in the room sounded so intelligent and on point, and how, when I could get something said, did it not seem to make sense even to me? I was, effectively, on mute.

To Elisa's credit, she kindly offered to take my few suggestions under advisement, but she was also quite firm in making it clear that I had overstepped my bounds. I don't remember how I got from that meeting room to my car, but I clearly recall the giant lump in my throat. I felt incredibly embarrassed by both my performance and the response. The meeting hadn't turned out at all as I'd hoped. I felt crushed and could barely get into my car before bursting into tears. Pretty quickly, though, the first wave of embarrassment turned into a second wave—this one of anger. The more I thought about it, the more furious I became.

I've been doing all of this for You, God! So, why did You leave me grasping for words in that meeting? How could You have let that happen to me?. . . I don't even think you are real, God!

This was, quite literally, the greatest smackdown of my life. I had acted pridefully in the past, but this was on a whole different level. It was probably the closest I had ever come to literally walking away from my faith, all because I had embarrassed myself. I knew that, deep down, there was more to my overreaction than embarrassment. I needed to do some self-reflection, but I wasn't even sure how. I knew I was going to try to figure out what had happened, though.

First, I bought a book at the Christian bookstore about how to be still. Next, I backed away from volunteer work and spent a lot of time on my front porch that summer, watching my kids ride their bikes up and down our quiet street or curled up in my favorite blue chair reading the Bible.

At first it seemed as if every verse I read was about how God disciplines His children because He loves them, or how He prunes the branches that don't bear fruit. I almost had to laugh, but I felt the deep truth of this and realized I was undergoing pruning. God was removing the dead wood, the prideful self-confidence I had been wearing like a fancy business suit and getting me into shape so that He could work in me and through me.

Eventually, I began to realize that, for me, the incident with MOPS had never truly been about our teen moms. It had been all about me and my deep-seated need to prove to the world that I was smart and capable and worthy. That I was good enough. Although I had considered myself a Christian for many years, that summer was the first time I truly surrendered myself to Christ and held myself out to be pruned. It was monumentally freeing—and also scary—to simply lay down my need for validation and tell my God that I was done fighting to hold on to what I thought my life should be and to instead give my life to Him.

I didn't know it then, but in teaching me to lay down my pride and my own plans, God was granting me a gift, preparing me for something bigger than I could have imagined, He was laying the groundwork for me to become a leader fully reliant on Christ. Out of that summer of learning to be still, a place called Hope House would be born.

John and Lisa with their children, Johnny, Nate, and Heather, 2002

7

This Might Be a Calling

Remember—the battle belongs to the Lord.

1 SAMUEL 17:47 (PARAPHRASED)

Tracey showed up almost every time our Teen MOPS group met. At nineteen years old and with twin girls just starting to walk, she needed the support! Tracey was always bubbly and friendly. She had a way of speaking that made her seem older than her years. Then again, she had been living an adult life for a long time. I knew that her mother hadn't been in the picture for years, but I wasn't really sure who Tracey had lived with since the age of ten. It seemed that she and her younger sister had been shuttled around a lot between family members.

Tracey got pregnant at age eighteen, but the father of the babies wasn't in the picture when she started coming to Teen MOPS a year later. Her daughters were the cutest little things, with dimples and brown-blonde curls, and Tracey obviously adored them. They had unusual names, which I had trouble remembering how to spell—Tracey had named them for characters in the movie *Men in Black*.

Tracey was one of only three girls who came to the Bible study we offered on the off weeks between Teen MOPS meetings. We couldn't find any studies written specifically for teen moms, so we had chosen a topical study written for moms in general, *What Every Mom Needs* by Elisa Morgan and Carol Kuykendall. The girls in the group related to the authors' personal stories about being moms and felt reassured to learn that all moms lose their patience, feel tired, and question themselves—not just teen moms.

Tracey asked a lot of questions and seemed to gobble up the stories about parenting. She was so eager to provide her girls with a better life than the one she had known—she just didn't have any examples to follow. There seemed to be very few healthy adults in Tracey's life, including the boyfriend she lived with, about whom I was beginning to worry. Tracey had mentioned that he had a temper, and I was shocked to learn that he was forty years old.

Tracey had grown particularly close to one of our group leaders, Debbie Espinoza. On Bible study week Tracey could usually be found next to Debbie on one of the couches in our church's fellowship room. I'll never forget the afternoon Debbie arrived before the girls and practically flew into the room, her contagious smile completely lighting her face as she shared that she and Tracey had gotten together the week before and that Tracey had decided she wanted a relationship with Jesus!

Now when we saw Tracey each week, she had a peace about her that I hadn't seen before. She was selling candles through a home party company, and she was good at it. She started making healthier life choices and eventually asked the boyfriend to move out. Tracey shared later that he was pretty angry about that, but I was glad she was becoming more self-sufficient and not relying on him as much. Her confidence seemed to be growing by the day.

Terrie Kearney was a woman with the gift of hospitality, and she loved a good home-based sales party, considering it an excuse to fill her living room with laughing ladies; her husband Ken would be forced to escape to the basement. I was just finding my footing with my faith after my summer of quiet time with God, and it felt good to be surrounded by friends from church and my co-leaders from Teen MOPS.

The evening was just winding down, and a few of our Teen MOPS leaders had stayed to help clear the dessert plates covered with brownie crumbs and drying chip dip. The last little knot of ladies was bathed in the porch light on Terrie's front steps, still laughing and calling goodbyes as they fanned into the warm summer night air to find cars parked around the periphery of Terrie's suburban block. I heard the screen door swing shut as Terrie came back into the kitchen, all smiles as she pulled her dark hair back from her face and grabbed her rubber gloves.

Amie and Karen gathered wine glasses, and Debbie and I helped dry and put away the dishes. Our talk turned to our teen moms and to one sweet girl in particular who was struggling because her mom had let a boyfriend move in, and they were openly doing drugs in the apartment. We couldn't find anywhere for this mom and her toddler to go, as she was just seventeen years old.

None of the shelters or transitional housing programs in the Denver metro area accepted minors. Local maternity homes sometimes housed minors facing a crisis pregnancy, but they wouldn't take a mom if she was already parenting. Debbie wiped the last glass with a soft towel and spoke a sentence into the warm kitchen air that marked the beginning of an entirely new path in my life.

"Well, maybe we should just open a home for teen moms ourselves."

There was a collective burst of voices, most of us laughing off the suggestion, but Debbie dropped her towel on the counter and turned to face us. "I'm serious. Our girls need a safe place to live; why shouldn't we provide one for them?"

We all talked excitedly for another hour, throwing out various ideas and scenarios. Terrie even threw out an idea for a name . . . Hope House. Driving home on that dark summer night, I had to admit that the sound of that name made my heart flutter a bit. I mentioned the discussion to John as we got ready for bed that night, still shaking my head over it. It sounded like an adventure, but ultimately it didn't seem very realistic. Little did I know that God was settling the idea into John's heart even as I was laughing it off.

Several nights later John arrived home from work, sending our golden retriever into frenzied excitement. School had started a few weeks earlier, but the late afternoons were still warm and sunny, and all three kids were outside playing. I was putting away the dishes from the dishwasher as John set his lunchbox on the kitchen table and pulled out one of the wooden chairs, dropping his hand to scratch the dog's head.

Intent on my chore and trying to figure out what to cook for dinner, I absent-mindedly greeted my husband. I admit to not paying much attention as he cleared his throat, clearly wanting to say something to me. I was stacking still warm plates but turned my head toward John.

"I was thinking while I was at work today about this idea of having a home for teen moms. It's weird, but I guess I got kind of excited."

Now John had more of my attention. My husband is a quiet man, usually pretty serious and not given to spontaneity. John is a careful thinker, a man of his word, and he doesn't make commitments lightly. "Excited" wasn't a word he used very often, unless he was talking about going on vacation. I set the plates down on our tiny kitchen counter with a clatter and turned to face John across the narrow linoleum floor, not sure what to say.

Before I could speak, he went on. "Actually, the more I thought about it, the more I started thinking that this might be a calling."

Now he really had my attention! In thirteen years of marriage John had never used the word "calling" before that day, and he has never used it in the years since. I abandoned my chore and pulled up a chair next to him at the table. My heart was suddenly pounding, and I felt a rush of combined excitement and trepidation. We sat and talked until the kids came bursting in, sweaty and red-faced from the heat of a Colorado autumn afternoon, demanding to know when dinner would be ready.

The following week John and I pulled into the church parking lot on a Wednesday evening, happy about the family potluck dinner, before sending the kids off to youth group and Pioneer Club. John and I were attending a new adult Bible study called *Experiencing God* by Henry Blackaby. There was a lot of homework, and we were on the week that describes how Christians often spend a good deal of time going in circles, repeatedly asking God to show us His will for our lives, when a better plan is to simply look around and see where God is already working and then join Him there.

We were learning how joining God where He is working can sometimes lead to a crisis of faith, as we must lay aside our own plans in order to pick up God's plans for our life. I felt as if I had been learning this lesson all summer long, but there were still some old priorities I was holding tightly to.

With the kids all in school, my dream of going to college was finally within reach. I hoped to become a teacher or to work in school administration one day. I had become very involved in my kids' school the prior year, even volunteering on a district-wide committee that was creating new content standards for curriculum.

I loved it so much and felt that I was making a difference. Plus, I was finally going to be able to say that I had beaten the statistic that only two percent of teen moms ever finish college. My sisters had both earned advanced degrees in law and medicine, and I was proud of them. I wanted to be able to say that I had gone to college, too. If I let myself admit it, I felt a bit ashamed that I didn't have a college degree.

I was also waiting for an invitation to come in the mail for a prestigious seat on another district-level committee for Jefferson County Schools. Somehow the fledgling idea for a home for teen moms seemed like something I could do on the side, while still pursuing the other things I was excited about.

That night in our Bible study class it hit me squarely that Hope House was not something I was going to be able to do "on the side." I knew that God was at work in the lives of our girls, and John had already decided that it was our calling to join Him there. I also knew that this would require so much more than volunteer work ever had. *Am I really willing to commit my entire life, outside of being a wife and a mom, to this thing called Hope House?*

The check that reads in the memo line, "May all our dreams come true," 2001

8

May All Our Dreams Come True

Each one will be like a shelter from the wind
and a refuge from the storm,
like streams of water in the desert and
the shadow of a great rock in a thirsty land.

ISAIAH 32:2

f I were being honest with myself, it wasn't just the idea of giving up my own plans that had me waking up in the middle of the night, my heart beating fast with both excitement and fear. The fact was that I could not conceive of a reason God would choose *me* to be a part of something that seemed so big and so far out of my experience level.

Also, deep down I knew He wasn't just calling me to be a part of this. He was calling me to be the *leader*. God didn't seem to be paying any attention to the fact that I had no college degree or background in social work and that my adult job experience included several years of being a home daycare provider and a sales associate at JC Penney's.

Ironically, the day after we learned about how a crisis of faith can actually be a part of the way God speaks to us, I received the packet of information in the mail about serving on the school district committee. The kids were in bed, and the house was quiet as I sat at our wooden kitchen table, the top scarred by years of craft projects and homework attempts. I turned the manila envelope over and over in my hands.

Can I do this? Should I do this?

My questions weren't about committee participation.

And in that moment, I knew the answer. *Yes.*

Yes?

Yes!

It took three repetitions, but after I said the final and definitive yes to God in my head, I tore the manila envelope in half and dropped it into the trash.

In the beginning there were four couples committed to the project: John and me, Terrie and Ken Kearney, Debbie and Allen Espinoza, and Amie and Tony Walton. The four of us ladies were leaders in the Teen MOPS group, and our families all attended Arvada Covenant Church together. We began meeting in the evenings each week, paying one of the older teenagers to watch Tony and Amie's kids, as their youngest was just a toddler at the time.

It was exciting at first, dreaming together at those meetings. We spent as many as twenty hours a week planning, studying what other homes across the country looked like, and speaking to community and church groups to share our vision. We wanted a place big enough for at least eight teen moms and their children, and we wanted Hope House to be more than a safe place to live.

We wanted to develop a program that would empower our girls to become self-sufficient, to finish school, to get a good job, and to build a career path. We wanted our moms to learn healthy parenting skills, to build healthy relationships, and to heal from the traumas they had experienced in childhood. In short, we wanted to give our teen moms the opportunity to break the generational patterns of poverty and trauma.

The thing was, we had no idea how to do any of that. What we did know was how to love our mamas. Through Teen MOPS we had witnessed firsthand how long-term, caring relationships had been the basis for incredible change in our girls' lives. Even though every single thing we were doing was new and had a steep learning curve, we knew that if we started with prayer and rooted our decisions in loving relationship we would be on the right path.

I turned to a woman I had met in our Experiencing God class; I didn't know her well at all but had learned that she was a gifted prayer warrior. One of our lessons in class had been around how God speaks to us through prayer. Sharron was probably in her mid-fifties with grown children—a tiny woman with short-cropped hair, wire-rimmed glasses, and a soft voice.

I called her literally out of the blue and asked if she would consider praying for Hope House and our little leadership team. To my utter surprise, she seemed delighted to have been asked and soon gathered a small group of prayer warriors ready to go before us in prayer, seeking wisdom for our decision making and ultimately willing to do spiritual battle for Hope House. But there was no way any of us could know just how difficult that battle would be.

Six months later, as our leadership group was gathered for a Christmas celebration, I received a phone call from a friend telling me to turn on the nightly news. It sounded as if one of our girls had been a victim of a domestic violence incident.

No, no, no, no . . .

In complete shock, all eight of us gathered around the television and watched as a picture of Tracey flashed across the screen while the newscaster calmly stated that a young mother had been killed earlier that evening by an estranged boyfriend who had then turned his gun on himself before police were called.

I felt numb, horrified by what she must have been through in those moments. The terror of that moment with my own dad and his gun came back to me in a flash. I shuddered at the memory. I had been lucky, but Tracey had lost her life and would never have the chance to grow up and pursue her dreams. More than ever, I knew that our teen moms needed a safe place to restart their lives and become strong and healthy moms. These girls needed us.

Just a few months prior to Tracey's death we had shared our vision for Hope House with the girls in our Teen MOPS group. The girls were so excited and anxious to help and wanted to know how soon we could get the home open. I was moved by their eagerness, which underscored the incredible need for stable, safe housing for this vulnerable population. We had asked our girls if they would be willing to participate in a video that we would use to tell the story and to highlight the complete lack of housing options for already parenting teenage moms.

Tracey had been the first to raise her hand. The morning of the filming, five beautiful girls and their children had crammed into the living room at Terrie's house. The video was filmed and produced pro bono by a wonderful gentleman from our church who spent hours shooting interviews with the girls and getting background film of the little ones playing together or cuddling with their moms.

The film of Tracey with her tiny twin girls would end up being the only video the little girls would have of their mom, who clearly adored them, laughing and cuddling with them in the background footage. It turned out that Tracey had hurt her back a few weeks earlier and couldn't work or care for the girls. Unbeknownst to our Teen MOPS leadership, she had asked her abusive boyfriend to move back in to help for a few days.

When she felt well enough to care for the girls, Tracey had asked her boyfriend to leave again, and he had become enraged. He ended up beating and killing her while her twins hid in a back bedroom. Afterward he would drive the twins to the apartment of Tracey's sister, Jenny, leaving them in her care before going out to the parking lot and shooting himself inside his parked truck.

Jenny, eighteen at the time, was working a full-time job at a local department store and barely making enough to pay the rent on her tiny apartment. We learned that she couldn't even afford to have Tracey's body released from the morgue to be buried. Shocked, our team scrambled together and pooled enough money to help Jenny pay for a small funeral and burial.

Jenny was heartbreakingly grateful, and even more so upon learning of the video we had of Tracey and her girls, as Jenny had very few photos of her sister with her children. Tracey's sister was eventually given custody of the girls. In a sad twist, Tracey would be buried just fifty feet from my little brother's grave.

Our fledgling Hope House leadership team was knocked sideways with grief and anger. I felt as if everything had been derailed. Some of our team weren't sure they wanted to continue the project, and we all felt there was little we could really do to keep our moms safe. *Who was I to have the audacity to think we could ever really change things for girls like Tracey?*

One night a few weeks later I woke up in the wee hours and lay there wide awake for several minutes. I had a full day planned for the next day, between the kid's school activities and a planning meeting for Hope House. I wanted to slip back into sleep but simply couldn't. I remembered my mother-in-law once telling me that sometimes God will speak to us in the middle of the night, when everything is quiet and we can hear Him better.

I got out of bed and pulled on my robe, trying to open our creaky bedroom door as quietly as possible so as to not wake John. Our golden retriever wagged his tail happily all the way down the stairs, sure that we were about to have a midnight adventure. I made a cup of Earl Grey with a bit of cream and honey and settled into a chair with my Bible.

"Okay, God, I'm here. What is it that you want to tell me so badly?"

I opened my Bible randomly to Isaiah 32, and my gaze dropped to verse 2. "Each one will be like a shelter from the wind and a refuge from the storm, like streams of water in the desert and the shadow of a great rock in a thirsty land."

It struck me that I had been hyper-focused on getting a *house* for the girls. I desperately wanted them to have a place where they could be safe from harm, and in my heart I felt as if I had failed Tracey by not having moved quickly enough to save her life. I sat and thought about those words in Isaiah, and it seemed to me that God was reassuring me that He had chosen *people*—our Hope House team, our prayer partners, our fledgling donors—to be a shelter for our girls. *We* were their refuge, their shade in the heat, their shelter in a storm. Not a house made of bricks and boards but the *people* He had called.

I read a bit further, and the verses went on to say, "Then the eyes of those who see will no longer be closed, and the ears of those who hear will listen. The fearful heart will know and understand, and the stammering tongue will be fluent and clear."

I grabbed my spiral journal from the end table next to my chair and copied down the verse in bright green ink. I read it over several times, and finally a truth began to form in my mind. *First, we will be their refuge*—our love, our care, our belief in them, would constitute their shelter. *Then their eyes would see and their minds would know the truth of God's love.* Tracey hadn't had a safe place to go when she had hurt her back and had felt forced to rely on an unsafe ex-boyfriend. But she *had* known God's love for her. She had found that among us, her shelter of Teen MOPS leaders and volunteers.

Into my mind flashed the check that Tracey had written back in September after I had hosted a candle party for her little business. Out of the profit from the home party she had made a gift of $15—the first gift from a teen mom for our ministry. On the memo line she had written one little sentence in her neat block print: *May all our dreams come true.*

I suddenly knew without a doubt why God had awakened me in the middle of the night. Tracey *had* had a shelter from the unrelenting hurt and chaos in her young life. She'd had us, and she had believed in us, and she had wanted more teen moms to have people in their lives who would be their shelter. We couldn't quit now.

I didn't quite grasp it then, but this was one of my first experiences with spiritual attack. Even the term "spiritual attack" had always seemed to me both religious-y and scary. It conjured up visions of battles with guns as in some dramatic action movie on the big screen where you couldn't even see the enemy in the dark.

I didn't understand then that Satan was evil enough to use the traumatic death of a young mom to depress me, weary me, discourage me, and make me question my right or ability to follow the call I thought God had given me. The verse "the battle belongs to the LORD" was coming into much clearer focus for me. The words of my mentor, Pastor John Tellis, started making more and more sense:

"When God gives you a little piece of His kingdom to be responsible for, and you carry that little piece of His kingdom, guarding it and nurturing it faithfully, He will entrust you with a bit more. And as sure as the sun will rise, if God gives you a bigger piece of His kingdom, the enemy will send a bigger army to stop you."

I knew then and there that there would be no turning back. We would continue the journey and rely on God to fight the battles, even—no, especially—the terrible battles. The next day I found the canceled check Tracey had written stored in our banking folder and made a copy of it. I slipped it into a cheap wooden frame.

I have carried that framed message with me for twenty years, sitting in a place of honor on every desk I've sat at while God has built His ministry from a twelve-bedroom home serving six teen moms to a campus serving hundreds of girls and children. I have never forgotten that message from Isaiah. No matter what God constructs in the form of physical buildings, what really matters will always be what He is doing with the people inside those buildings—the staff, volunteers, and donors who are the living, breathing shelter for our scared and lonely but determined teen moms.

The original residential house, 2003

9

I Will Bless You

Every good gift and perfect gift is from above,
coming down from the Father of the heavenly lights,
who does not change like shifting shadows.

JAMES 1:17

For the next several months our little team labored and persevered, determined to follow our call and open a home for teen moms. Finally, after several failed attempts to complete the IRS paperwork required to become a nonprofit, we wrote a letter to friends and family asking for support to hire an attorney we knew through church, Preston Branaugh, to assist us.

We made sure folks knew that their gifts would not be tax deductible and would simply be given in faith and in support of our dream. Finally, in June 2001 the day came when Preston called to tell me that we had received approval of our 501(c)(3) and that Hope House Colorado was officially a nonprofit organization!

Somehow, I thought that raising funds would become magically easier after we had received our nonprofit designation.

But by now we had been working on Hope House for an entire year but were still no closer to finding a home or bringing in the funds to purchase one. People were reluctant to give to a nonprofit that wasn't actually *doing* anything yet, even if the gift would now be tax deductible. Yet every time our team would start to feel discouraged, God would provide something new.

One Sunday we ran into acquaintances at church, the Andersons, and out of the blue they wrote a $1,000 check for Hope House! Even better, their daughter Kinsey had heard us speak in church and decided she wanted to give us all of the money she had received for her eighteenth birthday. I was so moved and encouraged by the selfless gift of a sweet teenager who recognized that she had something most of our teen moms did not—a loving family who celebrated and supported her.

Not long afterward we received a significant gift—a $5,000 check from Diane Halley, a woman from church who wanted to honor her late mother, Esther, who single-handedly raised three little girls in the 1940s after her husband left her. I was stunned and so encouraged. By now we had raised close to $20,000, but we were still a long way from having raised enough to rent a home or pay salaries. Then, in one of my middle-of-the-night talks with God, I read a couple of verses from Haggai 2:18–19:

"From this day on, from this twenty-fourth day of the ninth month, give careful thought to the day when the foundation of the LORD's temple was laid. Give careful thought. Is there yet any seed in the barn [any joy or hope in our hearts]? Until now, the vine and the fig tree, the pomegranate and olive tree have not born fruit. From this day on I will bless you."

I held onto those verses as a promise that God would soon bring to fruition all that we were dreaming of. Indeed, looking back, I recall that God actually introduced us during the third week of that September to David Nestor, the man who would one day donate something very big and unexpected.

I couldn't have known that then, though, and an entire second year went by as the four of us ladies spent days meeting people, sharing the story, and inviting others to join us. I absolutely loved getting to meet so many amazing people, many of whom are still today a part of Hope House!

Two years after beginning our journey together, both the Kearneys and the Espinozas decided that they were ready to move on from Hope House. Both had significant milestones taking place in the lives of their children, and both felt the time had come to focus on their families. Amie and Tony Walton and John and I were initially discouraged and spent one evening around my scarred kitchen table praying and asking God whether we should simply stop now or attempt to carry on.

Amie, the cheerleader among us with her contagious laugh and always sunny attitude, was the first to speak: "I say we just keep going as long as there is one single thing to do each day. The day that we wake up and there's not one thing on the to-do list, we will quit."

That evening marked a turning point, and we decided to move forward and focus on building a true board of directors. Amie and I were both determined to work at the house, once open, and we felt as though it was time to recruit, and also submit to, wise leaders.

John and Tony would remain on the board, and I knew the perfect person to invite to become our first Board Chair, Clarene Shelley. Clarene was the Chief of Investigations for a local police department and had both a strong, guiding faith and a depth of experience in working with at-risk youth and families in trauma.

Clarene was reluctant at first, mainly because she knew what a big job she would be signing up for, but once she had made the decision to become our leader things began to move. Clarene introduced me to a woman named Christine Bess, who had founded the local Court Appointed Special Advocates (CASA) organization.

Christine was tall, thin, and athletic, with a quick wit and a penchant for asking tough questions. She, too, joined the board, quickly followed by Roger Stapleton, a businessman who knew more about management and managing people than I could ever have hoped to learn. Our board meetings were now strategic and focused.

Looking back now, I can see how God had grown and moved us, preparing us and bringing us the right leaders before allowing us to actually open Hope House and fulfill the original vision by serving teen moms. I felt as if I were ready for that day when I received a memorable call from David Nestor, the man who had graciously met with Amie and me many months prior and who had been willing to share his knowledge as the chair of the board for Rocky Mountain Housing, an organization that builds supportive housing for at-risk families.

Amie and I brought David homemade brownies as a thank-you gift following our meeting with him, and he jokes to this day that we got our house because we gave him brownies. It turned out that David's organization had purchased several acres in unincorporated Jefferson County and that there happened to be a large brick ranch house sitting on the land.

David offered to let us move into the house and get Hope House started while Rocky Mountain Housing rezoned the property and annexed it into the city of Arvada. They planned to eventually tear the house down to develop a townhome village. The whole process could take a number of years, and they would charge us only $350 a month in rent, just enough to pay their insurance.

I remember calling Amie that December night, snowflakes swirling in the headlights as John drove us home from one of our kids' activities. I think I was laughing and crying at the same time, but Amie managed to make out what was happening. The miraculous news was sinking in—Hope House finally had a *house!*

It wasn't until the next day, as I shared the news with Clarene, that my excitement began to morph into terror. We didn't have sufficient money raised, certainly not enough for the full staff we would need to hire. And $350 a month in rent suddenly seemed like a lot! In reality I was just plain scared by the realization that, after all the planning, praying, and working, Hope House would actually be happening. Clarene called a board meeting, and the resounding consensus, despite my nerves, was that we would say yes to David Nestor and sign a lease for the big red brick home sitting in the middle of a field in unincorporated Arvada, Colorado.

On April 1, 2003, Amie and I stood in the kitchen of the former farmhouse with Preston, our attorney, and signed the lease. The house was completely empty and devoid of any furnishings but sparkling clean and smelling of Pine-Sol; one of our board members, Autumn, had come with her friends the day before to clean it from top to bottom. It felt completely surreal to sign a legal lease, my first real act as the new Founder and Executive Director of Hope House Colorado, a title that seemed much too fancy for me.

After nervously signing, Amie and I whooped around the kitchen and then started exploring the house, excitedly planning for moms to begin moving in. That night we gathered our board and our prayer team, and Sharron and Clarene led us in praying though every room of the house. It meant a lot to Amie and me, both having been teen moms, to be praying with our children in the living room of the house that their births had inspired.

From the very beginning God provided in the most amazing ways. My fear that $350 would be too much to handle in monthly rental expense? The first month we were in the house my son Johnny's friends threw a concert, headlined by his buddies' high school screamo band (a type of music I still don't quite get); although I couldn't understand the hollered lyrics, I certainly understood the heart and enthusiasm of a group of highschoolers excited to see Hope House become a reality. That night they raised $356.

The following month we received a gift for exactly $350 from Walt Anderson, whom I had never met and who didn't know what our rent payment was. He simply decided to give us the gift as a present commemorating his sixty-fifth birthday, after having learned about Hope House at his church. To this day Walt and Rita support Hope House and always bless my heart with their encouragement when I call to thank them.

Despite the many miracle gifts, my biggest fear in those early days was not being able to pay our bills, particularly payroll. This fear would literally keep me up at night. We had hired our first employee, Robin Scott, a petite blonde woman who had been a teen mom and had a passion for helping our girls. Robin and three other women worked part time to cover the House during nonbusiness hours, and Amie and I worked during the day, loving and guiding the programming for our first two residents, Tiffany, a sixteen-year-old whose baby had been born while she was living in a group home that wouldn't keep her after the birth, and Fendia, our eighteen-year-old mama from Haiti who had been unable to stay with family after they had learned she was pregnant.

In the beginning our finances were on a cash basis, meaning that we lived month to month. In reality that meant that we lived every-two-weeks to every-two-weeks, as payroll was paid biweekly. We had an incredible accountant, Mr. Palik, who ran our payroll pro bono and did our annual 990 for free (a 990 is the nonprofit version of annual tax documents).

I remember walking up the short flight of stairs in the building where Mr. Palik had his office, which always smelled clean and was full of sunlight. This man never had anything but a kind smile on his face and an evident sense of delight at being able to use his talents and his business to be a part of starting Hope House.

I always looked forward to seeing Rich Palik, but those trips to his office would often have my stomach in knots because there wasn't enough cash in the bank to cover the amounts printed on the paychecks I was picking up. There were months when Amie and I would hold our own paychecks, or not take them at all, in order to cover expenses.

Amie and I spent a lot of time devising fundraising strategies that mostly helped us avoid asking for money face-to-face. We focused on grant writing, not very successfully, and writing appeal letters, which did a beautiful job of telling the story but at first lacked specified fundraising goals or even a direct ask.

Our first fundraising event was a breakfast held in the basement of the church and dubbed the "Wassail Toast to the

Holidays" because my aunt was in charge of the food and décor and loved all things Victorian. We managed to raise $7,000, even though our silent auction bid sheets were cut from our kids' construction paper tablets, with lines for the bids painstakingly hand drawn using a ruler and a pen. It never occurred to us that we wouldn't be able to read half of the names of the winners when the breakfast was over because people tend to have terrible handwriting, especially when writing their name on a line.

My speech caused me two weeks of nervous stomachaches, but I got up behind the church podium and delivered an impassioned speech that clearly spelled out the enormous need for this ministry and how it would change the lives of teen moms in our community. At the end everyone clapped, and I felt a glow of satisfaction afterward, until a kindly older gentleman patted my shoulder and said it had been a lovely speech but that "it lacked a punchline."

I had told the story beautifully but had never asked for financial support.

Fendia with her daughter, Sarah, 2004

10

His Plans Are So Much Bigger Than Mine

Dreams come in a size too big
so that we may grow into them.

JOSIE BISS

God showed us plenty of grace during those early days. When we needed a microwave, someone showed up at the house with two. When we needed office furniture a neighbor let us pick everything we needed for free from his corporate office space before a planned remodel. When we were exactly $5,000 short of payroll, we received a surprise check in the mail for that exact amount from Ken and Diane Davis, who had learned about us because their daughter was a friend of my sister-in-law. Ken would go on to become a great mentor to me and even taught us how to plan and host a successful fundraising event. During that time I happened to be reading about George Mueller and the orphanages he had run in England in the 1830s.

I was encouraged by how God always provided after George prayed, including the time that there was no food at all for the orphan boys and George prayed fervently; hours later a horse-drawn cart arrived with a load of potatoes from a local farmer. In a twist that still makes me laugh and certainly highlights the fact that time is not linear to God, we ourselves would receive a truckful of freshly dug potatoes in May of 2020, when, near the beginning of a global pandemic, sixty teen moms each week were driving through our drop-in "Grab & Go" food supply line because grocery stores were closed or low on stock.

Ultimately, I was afraid to simply ask someone for money face-to-face. I was scared of what people might think of me and that they would say no. I learned a valuable lesson the day I met with a potential donor named Terry to give her a tour of Hope House. I vividly remember sitting with her after the tour and her turning to me with a gentle smile.

"You weren't even going to ask me, were you?"

Startled, I just looked into her brown eyes, and, before I could form a response, she said, "Lisa, you have to actually make the ask. When you ask people to give to Hope House, what you are really doing is inviting them to experience God through their giving."

To my amazement she broke out her checkbook and wrote us a check for $5,000. I was immensely grateful, not just for the much-needed funds but also for the incredible gift of wisdom that was the beginning of a change in my thinking about fundraising and a foreshadowing of what would one day become our fundraising philosophy when we adopted the principles of the Mission Increase Foundation.

My first true experience with how God can transform His people through their generosity came in the form of a slim blonde woman named Laurie Scott. Laurie was pretty, with a beautiful smattering of freckles, and had a friendly but reserved manner, but I couldn't quite tell whether she was interested in Hope House when she came for a tour with her good friend Terrie Ideker. Terrie was excited to have Laurie see what God was doing at Hope House and had invited her to get involved with the organization. Laurie had come because she loved Terrie and because her husband, John, was on the board of Terrie's family foundation.

Deep down Laurie wondered how she would ever connect with a ministry for teen moms. She and John did not have children, and even though John had lately been talking a lot about having come to faith in Christ, Laurie wasn't sure about this commitment. Having grown up feeling as if a person could never do enough to please God and should feel guilty for almost everything, she was suspicious of this supposed "freedom" and "relationship with Jesus" that her husband and Terrie often talked about.

Still, Laurie couldn't help but feel a pull on her heart when she met the teen moms at Hope House—especially Irene, who had come to Hope House at age seventeen with her sweet toddler son, unaware at the time that she was pregnant with a second child. Irene had grown up in a home marked by mental illness and poverty and had become pregnant and dropped out of school at sixteen. Now eighteen, Irene was determined to finish her GED and get a good job so she could care for Elijah in a way her own family had never been able to care for her.

When her mentor brought her for a visit to Hope House, and we told her that we had an opening, she was filled with wild hope for the first time in a long while. When she learned that she was pregnant again she was shocked, and even more so when she went into premature labor within days of learning of the pregnancy—at only twenty-nine weeks gestation. Little Neveah would be the tiniest surviving preemie in the state at that time, weighing only thirteen ounces at birth. Hope House staff spent countless hours driving Irene to the hospital to spend time with Neveah and supporting her as she navigated the medical system and made difficult medical decisions for her daughter.

Something about Irene's absolute determination to parent her baby well, while still focusing on Elijah, pulled at Laurie's heart. By the time Laurie came for that tour, Neveah had come home from the hospital, a whopping seven pounds at nine months of age, with life-sustaining oxygen tubes that would set off a loud alarm if Neveah's oxygen dipped to a dangerous level, which happened frequently. Yet Irene was calm and capable with her tiny girl—I picture her still with her dark hair pulled back and a perennial smile on her face despite her inner fears for her daughter's future.

When Terrie asked Laurie to help host a garden party to raise money for Hope House, she felt as if she had to say yes. She even volunteered to be in charge of the food for the party, which would be held in the stunning gardens of another friend, Judi Lundquist. Laurie spent hours planning the meal, calling caterers, and vetting menus.

She was anxious that the event go well, and by the day before the garden party she felt she had everything under control and could look forward to the party the next day . . . until a phone call from her chosen caterer doused her growing excitement. The caterer was cancelling their agreement and was unable to fulfill the order.

With sixty hungry ladies scheduled to show up in their summer finery to eat amidst Judi's abundantly colorful blooms, Laurie panicked. With her mind spinning around possible solutions, none of which seemed within reach, though, she had a thought. Maybe she should try this prayer thing that Terrie kept telling her about. After all, Terrie was always telling her some story about answered prayer at Hope House.

With this in mind, Laurie sank into a favorite chair, closed her eyes, and strove to quiet her thoughts. She tried to pull up some of the rote prayers of her childhood but finally settled on just a pleading prayer straight from her anxious heart: "Lord, I do not want to let these ladies down. More than that, I don't want to let Lisa and those amazing moms of hers down, especially Irene. They need this fundraiser, Lord, and they need for it to succeed, I need food—tomorrow! Amen."

Shortly after her prayer Laurie remembered a new restaurant she and John had tried and how kind the chef owner had seemed when they had met him during their meal. She picked up the phone and called Abrusci's, her heart thundering in her chest. She knew that the likelihood of this popular restaurant being available was slim.

She was shocked then when the chef himself came to the phone, listened to her dilemma, and without hesitation offered to make gourmet salads with chicken and cranberries, a house dressing, and plenty of Abrusci's famous bread. The chef even offered to deliver the meal to Judi's home and plate the salads for the party. Laurie got off the phone, relieved and stunned, and said a grateful thank-you prayer.

The garden party was a success, not only bringing together old friends for a fine meal but also moving their hearts to give generously so that Irene and the other mamas at Hope House would be abundantly blessed. Laurie was thrilled and enjoyed every minute of the party, and for days afterward she contemplated that prayer and how God had truly seemed to not only answer but to be *present* somehow.

She talked about her experience with Terrie and with her husband, and John encouraged her that this was the very Jesus he had been trying to tell her about. Laurie, still holding on to childhood ideas about religion, couldn't fathom a God who would care about her personally, even while she believed that He cared about our girls.

Day by day Laurie began praying a little more, and then one night she had a dream. The dream was so real that she felt as though she were awake. She stood in a garden, surrounded by flowers of every hue of pink. She faced a worn bronze gate standing open, and over the gate was a small cross, weathered and worn. She studied the cross and then realized that a man had walked through the gate and was reaching out to her.

The man wore flowing white robes and had the deepest, warmest eyes she had ever seen. She knew it was Jesus. She took a step toward Him and reached out to put her hand in His outstretched palm. As His hand closed around hers she awoke, realizing that she had been crying in her sleep. She knew without a doubt that she had met the living God and that, when He had invited her to come to Him, she had chosen to do so with all her heart.

Today when I hear Laurie, now one of my best friends and wisest advisors, retell her story and how Hope House has played a part in it, I still get chills. It is astounding to me that God is working through Hope House in so many ways—not all of them for the benefit of the girls and their little ones.

God's plans are so much bigger than mine, and His ways are so much higher than I can fathom. He is not only working *in* the lives of our girls but *through* them. There are a limited number of teen moms we will ever serve but a limitless number of people who can experience God through those girls and their stories. Which makes them not the victim, or the one who needs all the help, but the literal heart of a work that God is doing in a whole community.

I am awed by this truth and by the privilege of getting to be a tiny part of that plan, and today I love to invite others to experience God through their giving, having come to love our donors almost as fiercely as I love our mamas and their little ones.

The first ribbon-cutting ceremony at the residential house, 2003

11

You Can Have the House

*The LORD will watch over your coming
and going both now and forevermore.*

PSALM 121:8

I was just settling down into my worn office chair in the bedroom we had converted to a small office for our tiny staff when the call came. The girls were making breakfast, pans clattering on the stove and the smell of bacon in the air. Baby Sarah let loose with her signature shriek—never a cry but just a full-blown, ear-splitting squawk that announced her presence and demanded her mama's attention. I pulled the door to the office shut and reached for the phone.

David Nestor. I knew as soon as I heard the reserved note in his voice that I wasn't going to like what he had to say. "Lisa, our land has been annexed into the City of Arvada much more quickly than we had expected it to be. We're moving forward with our low-income housing development, which means that we'll need to tear down the house. You'll need to find somewhere to go pretty quickly."

97

I sank into my chair, donated just nine months earlier when we had opened our doors. My mind began spinning immediately. *I thought we'd have more time.* David's voice was kind as he asked me if we had begun planning for a move. We hadn't. Nine months had passed in the blink of an eye as Amie and I had focused on program development.

It turned out that what had looked great on paper needed a whole lot of tweaking now that we were working with real live teen moms. Not to mention the learning curves of how to manage our small staff, how to keep the books, and how nonprofit governance worked. I was frantically pursuing fundraising so that we could pay our staff and our bills, and there wasn't a dime extra for renting another house somewhere else.

I owed David the unvarnished truth. "We don't know what our next steps are," I admitted. "But we do have faith that God has a plan for us."

I said the last part mostly for David, because he felt so bad having to deliver the news to me, not because I really believed that there was a plan in that moment. I gently hung up the phone and turned to stare out the window at our little front yard, surrounded by the white picket fence that had been donated, three inches of fresh snow covering the sod we had laid in April when we had moved in.

It seemed like just yesterday that Fendia had moved in, toting a black garbage bag full of her belongings in one hand and a car seat in the other, ten-day-old Sarah, dressed in her only onesie, fast asleep. Nine months had passed, and Fendia had earned her GED and was taking college classes, working toward becoming an LPN. She had also become an American citizen after endless hours of studying the history, government, and geography of the U.S. I had quizzed her weekly and had learned more about American government studying with Fendia than I had ever learned in high school.

I felt the familiar doubt bubbling up. *What are we supposed to do now, God? Are we going to let these girls be homeless again?*

When Fendia had moved in, she'd had literally nowhere else to go. It hadn't been easy for Fendia since moving to the U.S. from Haiti at age twelve to reunite with a mom she hadn't seen since she was six years old. Fendia's parents had divorced, and her mom had immigrated to America, remarried, and had more children. As the political situation in Haiti worsened, Fendia's father decided to send her to her mom, intending to slowly move the whole family, as immigration law allowed.

Fendia had never before been on an airplane, and now she was flying to another country all by herself. She landed in Denver, Colorado, in the middle of a February snowstorm with no coat and only a rudimentary grasp of the English language to reunite with a mom she barely remembered and a stepfather she had never met.

It wasn't easy to assimilate into her own family, and when at eighteen she met a Haitian boy at a party, she simply wanted to not feel so alone. She was incredulous and terrified when she learned she was pregnant, and she didn't tell her mom until she was almost seven months along. Her mom, desperately worried about how her husband would handle something so far beyond cultural acceptability, asked Fendia to leave. With literally nowhere else to go, she had turned to a teacher at school, who had then brought her to Hope House. Now, just nine months later, I was about to make Fendia and our other residents homeless all over again.

The next few days passed in a blur. I alternated between wholeheartedly believing in God for an answer—some sort of a miracle, something only He could do—and fear, anger, and self-doubt. What had I gotten myself into? What had I gotten these girls into? Who was I to have thought for one single moment that I was capable of the task God had placed before me?

Every morning, I got up early to read my Bible before the kids woke up and demanded my attention. One verse seemed to stand out to me that week, and I grasped onto it: "The LORD will watch over your coming and going both now and forever more" (Psalm 121:8).

The next week Robin and Amie and I got to work making phone calls and searching for a place to go. This wasn't as easy as finding a house to rent, as we had to land in a place with the right zoning for a group home. So far we'd had zero luck, and I was back to panicking and waking up in the middle of the night. Somehow our girls didn't seem nearly as stressed as our staff, simply trusting that we would find a place to go together. If only I could trust God as easily as they trusted me!

Another week passed, and I was numbly performing the daily tasks the ministry required when the phone rang again. The house was quiet this time as I picked up the call. It was David, and this time he sounded excited. *I wonder why?*

"The board of Rocky Mountain Housing met last night," he said. "We've come to a decision. We want you to have the house." He went on to explain they were prepared to donate it to us, as long as we could pick it up and move it off their property.

I sat there, literally dumbfounded. My heart started pounding, and my mind began swirling with questions. *Is there even such a thing as a house mover? And where in the world will we move it to?*

I thanked David profusely and told him I would get back to him as soon as I could discuss the offer with our board. I sat back, still stunned, as Amie popped into the office for the teething gel we kept locked in a little medicine box in the office closet. She took one look at me and stopped in her tracks.

"What? What happened? Who was that?"

I repeated the words David had spoken.

We could have the house.

We just had to move it. By now I felt as if those words were imprinted into my brain.

Amie was instantly excited, whooping and hollering that it was a miracle. I was still stuck on the *how*, but Amie danced about the office, and the girls began crowding the office door, wondering what in the world was going on.

I sat quietly, feeling something moving deep within my chest, like a beam of light into a dark corner. *Hope.* God did have a plan. A crazy, God-sized, seemingly impossible plan. He was a mighty God, and He was indeed watching over our coming and going! I regularly had a plan of action and was always looking for the next practical step, but this time I was stunned. God was the One on the move, not me. I didn't know what to say.

Clarene called an emergency board meeting, and they made the unanimous decision to step out in faith and accept this crazy gift. One board member, Tony Scott, was a good friend of a realtor and asked her if she would help us find land to move the house to. She was so intrigued by the idea that she offered to work with us free of charge. We brainstormed ways to raise the funds to buy land and move the house, and Tony came up with the brilliant idea of getting a loan on the house. We owned it now, so we had an asset to leverage!

This was a pretty exciting idea . . . until I approached our banker, Hereford Percy, who was an amazing guy who loved our ministry but who definitely thought I had lost my marbles. I remember sitting in his office looking into his friendly but intense eyes, crowned by distinguished salt and pepper hair, and laying out the plan for FirstBank to give us a loan on the top half of the ranch-style home, since the basement level would naturally be plowed under when the house was moved.

"Naturally," he repeated, a rather stunned look on his face; I knew exactly what he was feeling. Hereford cleared his throat and sat back in his chair, straightening his coat and tie. "So, you're saying that you want us to get an appraisal on the top half of a house, which is going to have to have the brick removed down to the tar paper walls, the windows removed and boarded over, and a steel beam shoved under it to jack it up onto a truck? Lisa, I love what Hope House is doing, and it does seem like a miracle that you were somehow given a house, but this is not something I am going to get the bank's loan committee to agree to."

I immediately felt deflated and slouched down a bit in my seat. Then suddenly Hereford sat up a bit straighter, a slow smile spreading across his face. "But I do have an idea! If you can find a way to get a short-term loan with another lender, then FirstBank can come in and give you a traditional loan when the project is complete."

By this time Hereford's gaze grew even more intense, and I could tell the wheels were turning as he started processing what was happening to us. I was excited, too!

"Great idea! Now where on earth does one go to get a short-term loan?" I asked.

Since I didn't know where to start, and this was long before the days of Google, I turned to our board and champions. Someone sent me the name of a lender that worked exclusively with nonprofits who were attempting to mitigate homelessness; it was called Mercy Lending. Perfect! I should have known God would have a ready answer!

My first conversation with Sandy at Mercy Lending was an eye-opener. She was excited to give this a try but made it clear that this idea was outside of the norm. "Everything about Hope House has been out of the norm," I replied, undaunted. I couldn't know then that the process of getting that loan would be so immensely challenging. Every step of this massive project was way above my head. Part of me loved the challenge, but the practical, problem-solving side was completely freaked out.

I spent hours with Sandy during the loan process, often driving into downtown Denver to their fancy office building to deliver the next pile of paperwork she required. The day I finally went to sign the loan documents was so sunny that blinding light was bouncing off the glass on all the tall buildings. I finally found a parking spot that didn't require parallel parking, a skill I had never mastered. Getting out of my silver minivan, I straightened my skirt. I was in a pencil skirt and boots, my most professional-looking outfit, so I would feel like a grown-up businesswoman.

Once in Sandy's conference room, seated before a huge sheaf of loan papers and a pen, my bravado fell a notch. I clutched my written authorization from our board allowing me to sign for this loan. I vividly recall putting that pen to paper and signing my name in slow cursive, wondering how in the world I had come to be in this spot.

It was a bit like an out of body experience, watching a cool and collected thirty-four-year-old signing loan papers for what seemed like the huge sum of $100,000, while somewhere inside I still felt like an uneducated, inexperienced, naive teen mom. Part of me wondered if someone would pop out and blow the whistle on my inexperience.

An hour later I slipped into my sun-warmed car and carefully laid the folder full of approved loan papers on the seat next to me. With a whoosh I released the breath I hadn't realized I had been holding and just shook my head at myself and God.

Well, God, You have gotten us this far. I can't wait to see what You do next!

The residential house prepped to move to a new location, 2004

12

No Land to Put It On

I make known the end from the beginning,
from ancient times, what is still to come.
I say, "My purpose will stand,
and I will do all that I please."

ISAIAH 46:10

Our staff and board were so excited, and, frankly, I loved the adrenaline rush. We had gotten the money, and now we could take the next step . . . even if I had no idea what that next step would be.

The closest I had ever come to a construction project was painting my bathroom and putting in a new sink. Still, this was going to be fun! It turned out that there were indeed a few house movers listed in the fat yellow phone book, and I started getting quotes. Those bids popped my balloon fairly quickly, however, the least expensive being close to $40,000, almost half our loan money.

Meanwhile, our monthly bills and salary woes continued. As quickly as the miracles in the mailbox came in, a pay period would come and wipe them out. More often than not Robin and Amie and I were unable to take a paycheck ourselves. We had gotten a credit card with 23% interest rates and vowed not to use it except in emergencies, yet somehow there always seemed to be an emergency.

I found myself pondering something I had been reading in Nehemiah, an Old Testament book named after a biblical leader who also had an impossible call—to rebuild the ruined walls around Jerusalem, even though his people, the Israelites, were in rebellion. Nehemiah 9:33 stuck with me: "[God has] acted faithfully, while we acted wickedly." I thought about what Pastor John Tellis had said at a recent board meeting about our needing to get our financial house in order. Roger Stapleton had concurred, noting that a nonprofit is still a business, in many ways just like any for-profit business.

I was realizing that there was no earthly reason we should still be in business. God was keeping us afloat financially for *His* purposes, not because we were doing everything right. I wasn't sure what to do with that realization, but I was doing my best to turn it over to God and trust Him to show me how we could improve.

I was praying with our bookkeeper before we did bill paying, taking walks in the morning and hashing things out with God in my head as I walked around the lake, and trying at all hours of the day to literally picture myself leading the charge of what was about to happen.

I didn't know it at the time, but God did indeed have help on the way. My mother-in-law had recently introduced me to one of her friends, Betty Haligas, who would be coming for a tour of the house with her daughter, Terrie Ideker. As we moved through the kitchen, painted a warm yellow with our guiding verse, Jeremiah 29:11, stenciled over the doorway, I shared the logistics of the house move.

I talked about how the brick would have to be removed from the outside of the house, as it would be too heavy to lift otherwise. Steel I-beams would be run underneath the house through conveniently located windows on either end of the building, and then the structure would be gently jacked up from the concrete foundation walls to settle on those beams for a week prior to being hitched to an enormous truck and hauled off to its new home. Terrie asked if we had found a place to go while the house was being moved. "We are still looking," I admitted.

When the tour was over, I shared our recently made video, featuring three of our girls telling their stories of having nowhere to go and no family support and how God had given them not just hope for their future when they found Hope House but a *family* of staff and champions to rely on.

Terrie was so moved that she asked to borrow the video to share with her husband, as they had recently sold their gypsum supply business and formed a philanthropic organization called The Ideker Family Foundation. She wanted her family to get behind our project. Once again, I was stunned. Terrie's family had many connections in the building industry, as they sold the material used to make drywall.

Terrie asked to come to a board meeting with her husband, Doug; their two young adult sons; and John Scott, a financial advisor on the board of their family foundation. I was so nervous to present to their family, assuming that they were used to dealing with corporate professionals in big board rooms, so unlike our small but passionate board meeting in the living room of Clarene Shelley's house.

I wouldn't know until later that they had come to the meeting, mostly because Terrie had insisted, with little intention of buying in. I further learned that, after they had left the meeting, they had stood around their parked cars and prayed. Terrie's board had been moved by the passion of our board, especially that of my husband, John; Tony Scott; and Tony Walton. Doug shared later that he had never seen young men so dedicated to a ministry and not to their own egos.

However, their board knew that our little ministry needed far more than money. We needed—*I* needed—business mentors willing to invest a great deal of time into me. I truly believe that God loves to connect people, one to another, just as he weaves the stars into patterns in the night sky.

So, Betty brought her daughter; Terrie brought her husband, Doug, and their sons (one of whom would eventually chair our board); and Doug brought John Scott. Doug and John would become my wisest business advisors, challenging me often, though never unkindly, in everything from how I managed our budget to how I made hires to how I managed people. Coupled with Tony Scott, Roger Stapleton, and Christine Bess, they helped me get Hope House's finances in order.

As our business model became healthier, more people became attracted to our cause, excited to see the house moved and remodeled to accommodate more moms and children. One day I received a call from a man named Rory Norton, a general contractor who had heard about Hope House at his church when Amie had spoken there. He had been wrestling with God about his concern that he wasn't making a kingdom difference in his line of work.

"My business mainly consists of remodeling rich people's basements and dealing with their complaints along the way,"

Rory explained. He felt strongly that God was inviting him to join the work He was doing at Hope House.

Again, I was completely stunned when Rory offered to donate his time to be the project manager for our crazy project, while also feeling relieved that someone experienced in the work would take the reins. Rory and his wife had a young family at home, and I never was sure how he managed to pour so much time into Hope House, a project that would end up being a much longer-term journey than anticipated! But he wanted so badly to do something for God and to be a part of the work. With his bright blue eyes and little-boy smile, he radiated joy and a sense of purpose, as if he had been created for this project.

Now that we had a project manager, we needed a house mover and a piece of land to move to. Tony called a realtor friend, who immediately began a search for land. Next, we settled on a house mover, an experienced older guy who had been doing this kind of work for thirty years. He advised us that moving the house would be expensive and that we could move it only within about a seven-mile radius. Our realtor narrowed her scope and our budget to accommodate the tens of thousands of dollars the move would cost.

Then, in yet another God-move, a family came forward offering a beautiful, fully furnished townhome for us to move into while the house move and the remodel took place. The Rensink family would charge just enough rent to cover their own loan payment, which was frankly a miracle, as our most pressing worry was whether we would be able to keep our teen moms housed and moving forward in their programs while the building project was being completed. Rory expected the project to take about nine months after we had located the land to put the house on.

Looking back at our time in the Rensinks's townhome, we often laugh at the spectacle we must have made. We crammed five desks into the master bedroom and packed three teen moms and their little ones into the upstairs bedrooms. We had boxes of diapers piled up in the master bathtub, two chairs in front of the double bathroom sinks for staff meetings, and two more chairs in the empty master bedroom walk-in closet for counseling.

I was just starting to think this house move might indeed be possible, as Amie and I had spoken to every church, service club, and small group we could find, sharing our miracle and inviting people to become a part of it. We soon had a framing partner lined up through the Idekers.

Hap Lundquist, owner of Lundquist Associates, was willing to donate all of the labor and material necessary for reframing the house. Bruce Schock, a retired architect from my church, donated the architectural design. From a church just down the street came another miracle, as the owner of Tony V's Plumbing & Heating came forward with an offer to provide all of our plumbing, heating labor, and material. It couldn't have been going better . . .

Until I got a call from our realtor one evening. It was late, and I was already preparing for bed when the call came. As soon as I picked up I the phone, I knew from her voice that something was wrong.

"Lisa, I am so sorry, but there is simply no land available within your price range to move that house to. I can't find anything within a twenty-mile radius of you, let alone a seven-mile radius."

Her voice was soft and sad as she delivered a final statement: "We have to be done. There isn't anywhere to go."

I hung up the phone and sank down onto the bed in silence. Then I quickly became furious with God. I didn't have anyone to call, so I just let everything spill out to God. This was a problem so big I had no solution, no inspiration, no ideas. Strategy or sympathy from others wasn't going to fix this. Plus, I would have to tell everyone associated with Hope House that I had been wrong. The world would finally realize that I had no idea what I was doing.

What are You thinking, God? How could You provide so many pieces of the puzzle for this ministry to have a home of its own for our girls and their little ones and then withhold such a huge piece? Why on earth would You give us a house and no land to put it on?

From left to right: Robin, Lisa, and Amie on the land in Arvada where the residential house will be moved, 2005

13

The House That God Built

Unless the LORD builds the house,
its builders labor in vain.

PSALM 127:1

I woke up the next morning feeling numb and heavy—a lot like the feeling of grieving. I dreaded telling our little staff and our teen moms that we couldn't find a place to move the house. I felt a sense of betrayal from God, as I had embraced His promises and He had seemingly let me down. Yet I couldn't share those feelings with my team. They needed me to reassure them that everything was going to be okay, that God was in the midst of this.

I desperately wished that I could frame the news with a positive ending, to assure everyone that we had a plan, a place to go while we figured out what to do next, but I couldn't think of a single next step. I had no plan and no control over the outcome. I had to come to terms with the reality that the search for a place to move the house was officially over. I had no idea how to communicate that and still hold out hope.

When I arrived at the neat yellow townhouse, the inside was a swirl of activity, with moms finishing up breakfast dishes and zipping toddlers into coats so they could get to the amazing daycare center down the street that had reserved us a few free spots. Fendia was stuffing an anatomy textbook into her bulging backpack, and she looked up as I came in. We had gotten to know one another well in the last several months, and she at once sensed that something was wrong.

"Is everything okay, Lisa?" she asked in her lilting accent, a mixture of French Creole and English, and just the sound of her voice lifted my heart.

"Oh, just a busy day ahead," I replied, taking her heavy backpack from her so she could zip a squirming baby Sarah into her new coat. That baby girl had grown in the past nine months!

I wasn't ready to share yet. I wanted to reserve the day to think about the best way to talk this through with the girls. I jumped into helping with the morning rush and didn't step into my office until 10:30, just as the phone started ringing. *This had better not be a sales call*, I grumbled. *I'm not in the mood.*

"Hi, you've reached Hope House Colorado. Can I help you?" I answered with false cheer. A deep voice identified himself as Pastor Monty Newton of Heritage Community Bible Church. I had never met Pastor Monty, but a few older ladies from his church brought us laundry soap and cleaning supplies on a regular basis. I assumed he was calling in regard to a supply drive or volunteer opportunities. Instead, without preamble, Pastor Monty asked me a direct question.

"Are you the people looking for land?"

Startled, I answered, "Yes, we are."

"Well, we have some that we want to give you."

I wasn't sure I had heard him correctly, so I just sat there silently for a full thirty seconds before blurting, "What do you mean?"

"Well, I heard about your predicament from June Knight, who came to see me after she brought you all some laundry soap last week. She felt compelled for our church to somehow help you all. Now, we are not a big church, Mrs. Steven, and most of our folks are in their older years."

I rubbed the back of my neck. *What is happening?*

"I told June that we didn't have the money to do much for you all," the voice continued. "Well, Miss June said you weren't looking for money; you were looking for land. Mrs. Steven, we don't have money, but we do have a bit of land, and we want to give you some. We're just down the street at 64th and Benton. Why don't you stop by in an hour, and I'll meet you there?"

I could hardly breathe, and I know I definitely didn't say thank you. Instead, I mumbled a few words of agreement and dropped the phone back into its cradle, my hands shaking. I sat there staring at the phone, my mind blank, and barely heard the door squeak as Robin entered the room.

"Lisa? What's up? Who was on the phone?" Robin's big blue eyes were filled with concern.

I shook my head, still trying to make sense of what had just happened. "I think someone just offered to give us land."

"*Give?* As in free!? What are you talking about?"

"Pastor Monty, over at Heritage Bible Church, just called me. He said they want to give us land!" That was all I could get out. I sat, trying to take a breath, and then another, because I felt as if the wind had been knocked out of me. I still wasn't sure I had heard the pastor correctly, and my head was still spinning.

Within a few seconds Hope House and all of my hopes and dreams had gone from dead in the water to crazily alive. Robin didn't whoop and holler as Amie would have, but a slow, beautiful smile began to spread across her sweet face.

Robin was a slim, quiet woman with an innate wisdom that often helped guide our decision making when we were faced with one challenge or another from our teen moms. I counted her a blessing, as she had been a teen mom like me; although she was younger than me, she was innately both kind and practical.

"I know where that church is," she said now. It's the one down the street with a huge plastic Bible sculpture on their front lawn. Let's go check it out."

Just as Pastor Monty had indicated, the church was just four blocks south and one block west of our red brick ranch, well within our seven-mile radius. We made the turn onto Benton and saw a battered gold Toyota parked at the edge of a large field. Just across the field sat a beautiful red brick building with a cross-topped white spire rising into a bright blue sky. And there it was on the front lawn—a giant plastic Bible with the white pages wide open, gold rimmed on the sides, and black letters so big I could almost make out the Psalm from across the field.

Robin and I got out of my minivan just as the pastor emerged from the old Toyota. The irony was not lost on me that this man looked just like Santa Claus with a red nose, full white beard, and round tummy. His eyes literally sparkled as he introduced himself.

"Hello ladies. My name is Pastor Monty. Ladies, our church has been trying to put some sort of ministry on this land for a long time, and it has just never happened. We think God sent you here as a blessing to us."

Pastor Monty raised his arm and swept it toward the field. "We want you to have enough land for your house and a playground and whatever else you need."

I stood openmouthed, trying to take all of this in. Trying to breathe.

The pastor grinned. "Now I've gotta go to lunch, but let's get the ball rolling." With that he got back into his little Toyota and started the engine.

I stared after his departing car, dumbfounded. In that moment I was filled with a wild, rising hope. Robin and I stood there, looking at his car disappearing down the road and then looking at each other with big eyes.

What are You doing, God? Is this really happening?

A week later, after learning just enough to know that our next steps would be some sort of city approval for the land transfer and that things might not be as simple as they had first appeared, I stood in the Planning Department at the City of Arvada building with Robin by my side.

When Carol, the city planner, finally came to the counter where we waited, she seemed distracted and rushed. I tried to explain what we were there for. I knew she was familiar with the Rocky Mountain Housing project, and I figured she would be just as excited as we were when she learned that they had given us a house and that now we had a church willing to donate land!

Instead, she frowned behind her clear-framed glasses and shook her head, straight dark hair swishing across her round face. "I'm sorry, but this is not going to be possible. Rocky Mountain Housing has only a couple of months until they break ground. It will take at least a year to go through our zoning process to rezone the church property for multifamily residential use."

I immediately felt my heart sinking and the familiar argument with God beginning to bubble up. I started to sputter out a question when Robin laid a hand softly on my forearm. Looking directly at Carol, she asked what zoning, exactly, the land needed to have.

"You'll need an R-4 zoning."

"Could you go and check what the current zoning is? Just so we know?"

Carol sighed but walked across the room to a huge lateral filing cabinet and pulled open a heavy drawer. She slid through several large maps hanging in the drawer and finally removed a huge plat map of our northeast Arvada neighborhood and looked it over.

For a moment Carol just stood there, staring down at the corner of the map. From across the room even Robin and I could see the large green stamp in the corner: R-4. The map said R-4! I think that was one of many moments when God looked down at me and laughed just a little bit.

Incredibly, Heritage Community Bible Church had rezoned a portion of their property 25 years earlier, hoping to one day build a maternity home there. To this day I cannot help but get prickly eyed with tears when I think of that moment. Somehow, all those years ago, before I was ever even a teen mom, God had nudged the hearts of a church congregation, and they had responded in obedience, even though most of them would never see the house that God would one day put on their land. It was the most amazing example of how God really does perform miracles still today, and right in our own backyards. And He wasn't done yet!

From that moment in the City Planner's office, life became a whirlwind of activity. I would often recall the words of

Carole Davis, one of my mentors, who had founded and run a maternity home for teens, called Bridgeway, for thirty years. I was complaining to her one day early on, before we were open, about how long it was taking for God to get Hope House going. She told me to breathe deeply and enjoy these slower moments because soon enough I would be overwhelmingly busy. I should have listened!

At midnight on December 13, 2004, a group of us assembled outside the house on 69th and Sheridan. Sharron Neufeld came, and David Nestor, too. Our board was there, and so were most of our children, all buttoned into coats with winter hats pulled low. We stood in a little huddle excitedly laughing and talking, holding steaming mugs of hot chocolate in mittened hands.

Suddenly the giant jacks placed on either end of the house began to move, filling the night air with a low grinding noise, soon followed by great cracking sounds as the first floor of the almost fifty-year-old house was lifted from its foundation. All talking ceased, and I'm pretty sure I wasn't the only one who worried that the house might break in half.

A giant semi engine roared to life, and the driver began slowly backing an enormously long flatbed trailer underneath the house, guided by two coworkers at each corner of the home. At one point the peak of the roof appeared to be about to snag an overhead power line, and one of the house movers literally climbed atop the roof and straddled the peak, holding the wires up in a gloved hand while the trailer inched forward. Finally clear, the trailer bumped gently over the curb and out onto Sheridan, preceded by the flashing red and blue lights of a police escort.

A great cheer rose from our little crowd. *This is happening. Hope House is forever! And so is this little group. This isn't just my dream—this is* our *dream.* I looked over at David Nestor, usually so reserved, jumping up and down with joy in his button-up wool coat and newsboy hat, somehow still looking very dignified with his silver hair and wire-rimmed glasses. He was just as much a part of this as I was.

We all piled into cars to follow our house in a midnight parade for the short journey to the field near the church, where the trailer would be parked and the house would sit, waiting for the next phase of its journey. God was moving mountains— things that weren't supposed to move. But He was doing it.

What happened in the following months could only be described as an old-fashioned barn raising. While we had money left from our loan, we had learned that the costs of the underground sewer and plumbing alone would far exceed our nest egg. The only way we could remodel our house was if the community would come together to make it happen.

Doug Ideker reached out to Joe Coors, who agreed to donate the money for the underground infrastructure but, more importantly, agreed to be on our advisory council.

Joe was an incredible businessman and strategist and would become one of my wisest advisors. He also loved the game of golf, and over the years he helped develop our golf tournament into a very successful fundraising event, which would eventually be renamed in his honor following his passing in 2017. Most of all, though, Joe loved the Lord with all his heart and wanted so much for our girls to know that God loved them and had a plan for their lives.

Rory seemed to have an endless list of things to do next, which we never had the money for. Fortunately, God just loves to invite people to become a part of something bigger than themselves, and that's exactly what He did. Sharron's husband, Don, introduced us to Kelly Spencer, who owned an excavating company. Kelly volunteered to excavate our basement. Suburban Reddi Mix stepped forward to donate all of the concrete necessary for the foundation walls, and an introduction to a man who worked for Adolfson & Peterson, a large construction company in Denver, led to the donation of our structural steel.

It might seem strange, but I absolutely loved asking for the things we needed to build our house. We had momentum! Rory would call and tell me what we needed, and I would ask him what exactly it was, how to spell it, and where to get it donated from. Everyone was so excited to be a part of our project.

When our case manager, Michelle Gonzales, told one of her friends about it, his roofing company decided to donate our roof, which eventually led to their donating one roof a year to charity because they'd had so much fun with Hope House.

One day Rory told me we needed thirteen four-foot egress window wells. I reached out to the company Rory directed me to, and the manager told me they'd just had an order for fourteen window wells cancelled and would be happy to donate them to Hope House! Some days it felt as if I would pick up the phone and find it a direct hotline to heaven.

On other days my faith would falter, usually around a challenge that seemed impossible to get past. When we learned that the city would require us to have a $50,000 escrow account in case we were to damage city streets and need to repair them, I just about had a fit. *We don't have $50,000 just sitting around to use in case of a crack in the road!*

But Robin, ever my calmer counterpart, told me that I should write a letter to the city and ask if they would reconsider. Fuming,

I sent the request, sure that it would be denied. A week later I received a letter from the city with just one line printed on the city letterhead: "Your request for a waiver from escrow is approved," signed by the city manager. I almost cried. Still, every time we experienced a miracle we also seemed to encounter a roadblock.

Pastor Tellis reminded me often that God doesn't make a promise He doesn't intend to keep. I relied on those words when the day finally came to move the house onto its new foundation. What should have been a celebration became a disaster, though, when the house mover made a major mistake and hauled the house right across an underground ditch in the church property, breaking the ditch in two.

In Colorado, ditches can be privately or individually owned, or they may be "mutual," incorporated ditches. Water in the incorporated ditches is allocated by shares issued by the company and represents water rights, so breaking a ditch was a big deal. The house was safely on the foundation, but there wasn't anything we could do about the ditch other than fix it. As a result, we were left with an $8,000 bill for Juchem Ditch Company to repair that ditch!

Then in August 2005, just as we had the house "dried in" and were able to start the electrical and plumbing work, Rory decided to step down. I couldn't blame him, as he had a growing business to operate and a family to feed, but this was certainly a blow. We were eight months into a project that was supposed to take only nine months but was nowhere near completion. Our loan from Mercy Lending was a one-year loan, and we'd already had to ask for one extension. And we needed to complete renovations on the house so that we could finalize the permanent loan from FirstBank and pay off Mercy Lending.

I was in a near panic, but God, as usual, was ordering our steps. One of our amazing employees, Tara Cox, reached out to her stepdad, Fran Mundt. Fran was a carpenter, and he agreed to pick up where Rory had left off! He was sure he could get the project done by the end of the year.

Fran was a miracle worker, and the house was finally beginning to look like a home! The windows had been installed, and the house was now filled with light when I made my daily visits to check on progress. Fran built windowsills, installed handrails on the stairs to the basement, and laid donated floor tile.

Another amazing volunteer, Marv Giddings, was at the house daily. Months earlier we had learned that we couldn't reuse the original brick that had been removed from the house before it was moved. Marv had gone to bat for us, getting brick and masonry donated.

Now he came to help with any odd job Fran had for him. Still things were moving slowly, with only the two of them and an occasional assist from Tom, an older gentleman who loved to stop by and volunteer.

We inched our way into 2006. I had started getting calls from Mercy Lending. They would give us until June, at which point we *must* have permanent financing in place. I knew I would need two months for FirstBank to complete their loan process so I could have the funds by June, and that meant that the house had to be completed by April.

By mid-February the situation was reaching a critical point. The carpet still wasn't laid, the paint wasn't done, and the doors weren't hung. Roger Stapleton, our board chair by this time, called an emergency meeting. It was time to call in the troops!

I put out the word to every volunteer, donor, and church that had ever participated in Hope House in any way, and, once again, God seemed to open the heavens. A professional house painter stepped forward to paint. An old friend from MOPS, Elizabeth Melvin, sent her husband and son, who had carpet-laying experience. The two of them worked ten-hour days to get the carpet installed by the end of March.

On April 1 a crew of volunteers and board members descended on the house. John and Roger installed baseboard. Christine Bess brought her husband, Brian, and their two teenagers, Conrad and Morgan. The Bess family filled in about a million tiny holes where the nails had been driven into the baseboard and painted over each one. Tony's crew hung the doors. A friend from Arvada Covenant Church, Brian Thies, secured window coverings and had them installed.

By April 8 we were ready to move in the furniture. All we needed now was the green light from the city of Arvada, but they still hadn't approved our certificate of occupancy because they were waiting on the plumbing inspection.

My stress level was at a boiling point, and to top it off my mother-in-law, Michele, had begun feeling unwell again. It had been several years since she had undergone her first kidney transplant the night before our wedding, and she had been loving her new lease on life, which included as much pumpkin pie as she wanted now that potassium was no longer a fatal danger.

Unfortunately, it looked as if that kidney was finally failing. Michele was as much a mom to me as my own mother. When Johnny was born, knowing that I had no real friends she had hosted a baby shower and invited the Fenton Street Gang, *her* best friends. When Johnny was finally potty trained, she had baked a cake and invited the family over. Through the years she had celebrated my kids, encouraged my marriage, and led me in growing my faith.

Now she was having a second kidney transplant, and this time the kidney was being donated by John's brother and best friend, Scott. While our family waited nervously on lime green upholstery, silently praying for our mom and brother, my cell phone pinged. I jumped, annoyed with myself for not having turned off the phone. Glancing down, I saw that the number was that of the planning department at the City of Arvada. Quietly excusing myself, I moved out into the hall, sneakers squeaking on the linoleum floor.

"Lisa, it's Carol Ibanez at the city." Carol's usual cautious reserve had been replaced with excitement. "I just got the word. Your certificate of occupancy has been approved! You can move your girls into the house!" I could have whooped in the quiet hospital hall from the release of stress her words brought me, but I saved my exuberance for the news of a successful surgery for both Scott and Michele a couple of hours later.

On Saturday, April 15, 2006, the teen moms of Hope House and their children finally moved into the newly relocated and renovated home. Tonya's three-year-old daughter was so excited that she kept bouncing off the living room couch, running down the long hallway with bedrooms on either side, and racing back to do it all again. The little ones had been so cramped in our rented town home, and having 5,500 square feet of house to run in, plus a beautiful front yard to play in would be a welcome change.

The yard was bordered by a little white picket fence surrounding the new sod carefully laid out by many volunteers. There were new flowers and shrubs and a new play structure donated by a church. I stood, watching the kids gleefully running around the front yard or riding trikes down the ADA ramp and collapsing into the grass. "This is *mine*?" one little girl asked, eyes big. Such joy I felt!

In what was surely no coincidence, the very next day was Easter Sunday, and the first meal prepared in our brand-new kitchen was Easter dinner. I stopped by the house to see how dinner was going and again experienced waves of joy and a sense of completion and relief. We had carried out the work God had given us to do, with much help. I felt a sense of peace.

This is done.

This is good.

Then, this: *Look what God can do!*

Danielle with her daughter, Gracey, 2011

14

If There Is a God,
He Hates Me

Why are you so far away when I groan for help?
Every day I call to you, my God,
but you do not answer.

PSALM 22:1-2 NLT

Danielle, one of the first teen moms we interviewed after moving into our forever home, sat hunched in the chair in our meeting room as her tiny body curved protectively around her tight, round belly. She was sixteen and close to her delivery date and looked very much like the child she still was.

One look at Danielle's face, though, dispelled any misconception about childlikeness. Danielle wore her makeup like a shield, applied with a heavy hand and designed to make her look more grown up. It would be several months before I would see her beautiful face free of thick foundation and discover that she had a pretty smattering of freckles across her nose and cheeks. For now, those gorgeous freckles were concealed.

What really struck me that day were her eyes, a startlingly bright blue green, which currently flashed defiantly as she answered interview questions designed to determine whether she would be a fit for the Residential Program. Her little body was tensed like a cat ready to spring, but underneath her defiant exterior I sensed strength and determination—and also a great deal of fear.

We would learn that Danielle had been adopted as a baby by a loving middle class couple. Her early childhood had been almost ideal, with trips to visit members of her family who held high-level positions in the military and a family vacation to Paris one year. Everything in Danielle's world had changed, however, when her mom's drinking had become excessive. When her parents thought she was asleep they would break into huge fights, leaving her scared and sleepless.

At thirteen Danielle was blowing into the breathalyzer in her mom's car for her so that her mom could drive her to school, still drunk from the night before. Her mom became physically abusive with Danielle, prompting school calls to Child Protective Services. A final incident occurred when Danielle's mom pushed her face into the dashboard of the car while driving, leading her dad to make a CPS call and finally file for divorce.

By the time her parents split up, Danielle was getting into minor trouble with the law, and her dad had no idea how to deal with his furious little girl, and at fifteen Danielle was placed in a temporary foster home. To Danielle the situation felt anything but temporary. She felt abandoned and terrified, and she channeled those feelings into anger and destructive behavior and relationships. Her constant companion in most of her troublemaking was a boy who also had a broken family and who shared her penchant for wild adventure.

Despite her hard, seemingly confident outer shell, Danielle felt completely out of control inside. When she became pregnant at fifteen, no one was surprised. But for Danielle something very important shifted. Her baby became a reason for her to live, and to live differently. Danielle began focusing her considerable energy into changing her life and planning for her baby. She no longer dwelled on her own feelings of abandonment but began to concentrate on how she could protect and provide for the baby she carried.

The reality, though, was that for a girl like Danielle there were very few choices. Her due date was coming near, and the licensing of the group home she lived in made it impossible for her to stay there after the birth of her baby. At barely sixteen, Danielle faced the almost inevitable reality that she would be separated from her baby at birth and they would be placed in separate foster homes.

Danielle had called every place in the phone book, every shelter, every transitional housing program, and talked to every case worker who would listen to her, but there simply weren't any housing options for a parenting teen mother in Denver. Finally, during a late-night web search Danielle happened upon a site for a place in Arvada called Hope House. Wrapping a slender arm around her growing belly, Danielle felt a tendril of hope taking root.

Now she sat in our meeting room, her social worker from the group home by her side, and listened as we gently informed her that she would have to be parenting in order to apply for our Residential Program. This meant that she would have to give birth and make the decision to parent before she could move in. Every cell in my body wanted to bend this foundational rule and allow this scared, determined, and clearly intelligent young girl to move into the beautifully furnished bedroom down the hall from where we sat.

For a moment I teetered on the edge of blurting out that we could make an exception. After all, I was the Founder & Executive Director; if anyone could make an exception to a policy, it should be me. But I bit the inside of my lip and took a breath as I looked at Amie across the room. Her eyes were welling with tears of sympathy, and I could see that she would back me up if I were to make the exception.

It honestly took everything I had in that moment to look this beautiful girl in the eyes and tell her what I had to. "Danielle, we have to abide by the structure of our program. When we developed Hope House, after a great deal of thought and discussion, we made the decision that we were not a maternity home."

The very heart of our mission was to help *parenting* teen moms to become self-sufficient, and there was a reason behind that early decision. A pregnant woman, no matter her age, simply can't know how her world will change in the moment her baby is laid in her arms. Teenage mothers in particular are wrapped up in the chaos of their lives and have unrealistic thoughts that the birth of a baby might heal all of the difficult relationships they are involved in.

Yet when that baby is born, and what we have come to call "mommy motivation" takes root deep within a teen mother's soul, there is almost no amount of chaos in her world that will keep her from building a better life for her baby than what she herself had grown up with.

Being the leader is hard. It takes so much discipline to say to your own self, *It's not about you; it's not about how your heart feels.* I wanted to make a decision based on sympathy and mercy, as I would several months later for the Vang sisters. In their case I would make the decision to bring them into the house after they had been sleeping in the park out of pure heartbreak for them. In that case we would not go through the usual intake process.

But taking in Danielle prior to her baby's birth would not have been a process exception. It would have been a mission exception. In that moment, in our little office sitting across from a girl whom I would come to love dearly, I felt a great appreciation for our mission statement. It had taken several frustrating months of board discussion and endless wordsmithing to come to a final version:

> Hope House Colorado empowers parenting teenage moms
> to strive for personal and economic self-sufficiency and to
> understand their significance in God's sight, resulting in a
> healthy future for them and for their children.

Helping *parenting* teen moms is our mission, and as the leader I had to align my decision making with our mission, not my own heartstrings. I was the person who could say yes or no: I could bend the rules or even change them. But even though my heart wanted to make an exception here, it would have been the wrong decision. I needed to rely on my head and follow the process, because for Danielle that would be for the best.

Danielle left our office disappointed but not crushed. The girl had grit and determination even at sixteen. Danielle's social worker was determined to help her move into Hope House and found her a temporary foster placement with a couple who would end up becoming lifelong friends and mentors to her. They supported her through Gracey's birth and helped her move into Hope House when Gracey was just three weeks old.

Danielle's father, who still had legal custody of Danielle, signed the paperwork required for her to move into our program. As her father, Danielle's dad was acknowledging that he retained all medical, financial, and legal responsibility for his daughter, while giving her permission to live at Hope House and participate in our self-sufficiency program. Our intake paperwork clearly spelled out the fact that our program was voluntary and that Danielle's dad would be responsible for her housing and care if she should choose to move out of Hope House.

Danielle was every bit the spitfire I had seen during her interview. She tackled everything our program required with energy and an underlying spirit of fun. She was articulate and bright and had a sharp wit, often causing staff members to burst out laughing at her sarcastic humor. On the flip side, Danielle was stubborn and bold, and if she didn't like a rule or a decision made around her program, she wasn't one bit shy in stating her opinion on the matter.

Going to church was one of those things Danielle pushed against. In all areas of our work we seek to share the love of Christ with our girls. Many of our girls come to Hope House believing that, if there is a God, He must either hate them or be mad at them; why else would their lives be so hard? Some have had painfully judgmental experiences at church during their pregnancies, or with family members whose faith traditions are harsh and rigid.

For these girls hurt and shame are deeply rooted, impacting their sense of self-worth in incredibly damaging ways. For some teen moms God is a distant, angry figure who stood back and allowed horrible things to happen to them as children. For them, a sense of abandonment and fear guides their perception of God. Our girls have a tremendous longing to simply feel loved and valued, but very rarely do they know that this is exactly how God feels about them.

Everything we do at Hope House is born out of our deep conviction that God loves us and that nothing we have done, and nothing that has been done *to* us, causes God to stop loving us or to stop having a plan to give us hope and a future. This is our belief for every teen mom, child, staff member, donor, and volunteer. This is the heartbeat of Hope House.

This abiding love and hope are reflected in the pictures hung on every wall, huge, colorful photos each capturing one of our moms in a moment of joy with her little one, smiling, laughing, and glowing. They are reflected in our warm greetings when a teen mom, volunteer, or champion walks through the door, because we are truly glad to see them.

You can just *feel* God at Hope House in a way that is hard to explain. It is so critical that our girls and our donors both have an opportunity to bump into Jesus at Hope House—not some condemning, angry, distant God but a God who sacrificed His only Son to connect us back to Him because He doesn't want to live without us.

Danielle fell into the category of assuming that God was mad at her . . . which was fine with her, because she was just as mad at Him. She went to church with her housemates only because she had nowhere else to go and the girls weren't allowed to stay alone in the house without staff members present.

Many of the girls were attending a huge church called Flatirons Community Church. They loved the rock and roll music and the fact that they could show up to church in jeans. But mostly they loved the "Me, too" message that we all have "stuff," things we have done or things done to us that make us assume that God doesn't want us . . . until we actually bump into Jesus and experience His grace.

For months Danielle put in her headphones and listened to her own music from the moment she slouched down in the chair at church. Then one Sunday, out of boredom, she decided to listen to the pastor teach. She was intrigued but still angry. *Who was this God the pastor kept talking about? Why did the guy keep insisting that God can work in and through us? What did that even mean?*

Something in the message must have been sinking in, though, because she stopped taking her headphones to church. She started asking more questions at the dinner table and began plopping down with a staff member when they led devotions at night before lights out. Several months after pulling those headphones out at church, Danielle would get a cross tattooed on the back of her neck with the date that she had decided to accept the gift of God's love for her.

A few weeks after that she walked down the aisle at Flatirons Community Church with Anne and Tina Vang to be baptized, an outward display of their inward decision to love and follow Jesus. Years later Danielle told me the story of how that moment had come to be for her. She told me how angry and scared she had been when she first came to Hope House and how she didn't believe for one minute that we really cared about her the way we said we did.

Then came the day that Anne and Tina Vang showed up in the kitchen, disheveled and exhausted after having slept outside in a local park. She said she watched us feed them, comfort them, and love them. Something broke through Danielle's anger that day as she witnessed faith in action for the first time in her life.

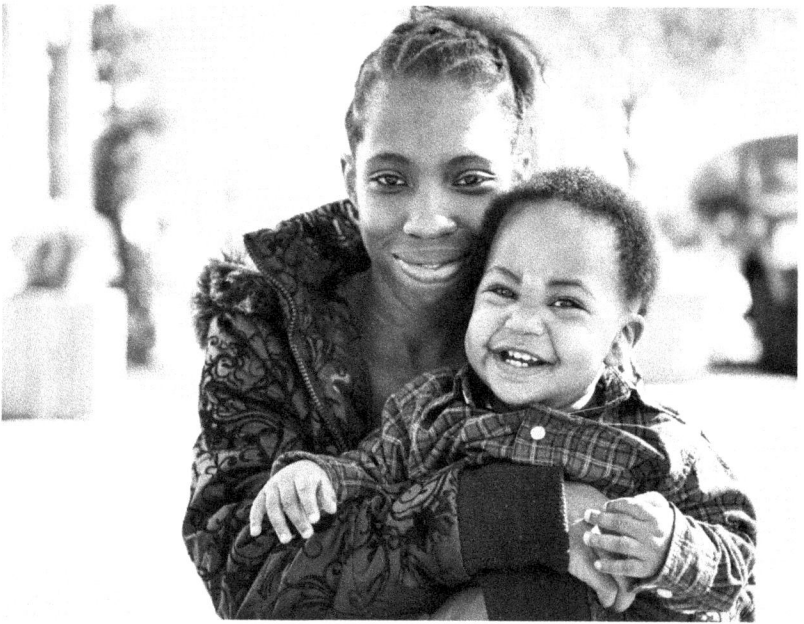

Chantia with her son, Omarion, 2011

15

Learning to Let Go

*For I know the plans I have for you," declares the L*ORD*,*
"plans to prosper you and not to harm you,
plans to give you hope and a future."

JEREMIAH 29:11

Word about Hope House began to spread, and we were receiving dozens of calls each month from teen moms who didn't necessarily need a place to live but who needed support in moving forward in their lives. The ministry had been growing steadily and serving more girls since the board had made the decision in 2007 to expand beyond a Residential Program and begin serving teen moms in the greater community.

Our Parenting Educator, Shannon Jenkins, was particularly moved by those phone calls from teen moms. She had a vision for how we could expand and begin serving more teen moms. Shannon and Amie spent months researching and developing a mentoring program focused on self-sufficiency, with the idea that a volunteer mentor could help her teen mom with school and job preparation and in making healthy relationship choices.

We soon had a dozen matches made and a list of ten more girls waiting for a mentor. It felt a little like being back in Teen MOPS, gathering those moms at the house or at a local park for meetings with their mentors and learning how hard they were working to build stable lives when faced with seemingly insurmountable challenges.

We were shocked to learn that most of the teen moms in the Mentoring Program had dropped out of school by the ninth grade, often because their high school wouldn't accommodate absences for morning sickness or recovery time following the births of their babies or because they simply couldn't find childcare. Most of the moms had had what we would come to call an interrupted educational experience. Growing up in generational poverty, these girls had moved around a lot and had often been enrolled in eight or nine schools before the ninth grade.

In 2008 we made the decision to start a GED Program and promoted one of our residential advisors, Elizabeth Corless, to GED Coordinator. We partnered with Heritage Bible Church next door for classroom space, and they allowed us to take over two unused Sunday school rooms, painting, decorating, and bringing in computer tables and laptops.

Our GED Program offered one-on-one tutoring with volunteer tutors, and I loved watching the girls blossom with the individual attention they received. I'll never forget the day when Chantia joined the GED Program; this scared young Black girl came to class only because she loved her mentor and wanted to please her.

Chantia had grown up with an alcoholic mom and an abusive dad, and school had been hard for her, not because she wasn't capable but because she was often forced to escape her home, sometimes sleeping outside before going to school. She had dropped out in the eighth grade after a teacher had told her she was too stupid to learn.

Chantia had internalized those cruel words and believed them to be true . . . until the day her tutor, Craig, watched her do a math problem and told her in his booming voice that she was *so* smart. "Look what you can do, Chantia! I can't wait to be at your GED graduation one day soon!"

Something as simple as a grown-up's encouragement can be utterly life changing for our teen moms. Six months later Chantia marched proudly down the aisle of Trinity Baptist Church in her cap and gown to the strains of "Pomp & Circumstance," Craig sitting proudly in the audience for one of our first-ever GED graduation ceremonies. My heart was popping as I sat up on stage and watched Chantia glowing with pride. Her mindset had completely shifted; she was a young woman who had once thought she was stupid but now knew differently, and had hope for her future.

When I stood up to address Chantia and the others, I looked out across the church filled with friends and family members dressed in their best clothes, much like most any other graduation ceremony. I then looked down at the row of teen moms, graduation caps perched on curled hair and high-heeled shoes peeking from under their gowns.

"I am *so* proud of you! You accomplished this! You earned your GED, overcoming barriers that most high school students have never faced. You studied late into the night while your baby slept. You took the bus all the way across town to get to Hope House. Many of you earned your GED while also working and helping care for family members. Your hard work and dedication are such an example to your little ones. And this is just the beginning, for "He who began a good work in you will carry it on to completion until the day of Christ Jesus" (Philippians 1:6).

By 2009 we were serving somewhere around forty teen moms a year, and we had added staffing to coordinate the Mentoring Program and the growing GED Program, as well as an administrative assistant to support us all. We had even begun looking for a new location for our offices and the GED Program to move to. It had become so crowded with staff at the house that we had taken over two bedrooms as shared office space to house our growing team. The GED Program was now operating out of three classrooms at the church; still, as generous as the church was, we longed to find a space that we could really make our own.

I reached out to Doug Ideker, one of my wise advisors, and laid out a plan for leasing new space and ramping up administrative support. He cautioned me that we might be moving too quickly, but I wasn't really listening. I just wanted a stamp of endorsement. I moved forward in recommending a 2009 budget that included leasing office space, and the board somewhat reluctantly approved it.

By the beginning of February, I was becoming concerned that I had indeed led us to bite off more than we could chew. It was clear that I should have been paying closer attention to the many news stories about the looming national financial crisis, the "housing bubble burst," and what would come to be called the Great Recession.

Our gifts had slowed to a trickle. We had just enough savings to pay bills and payroll on February 15, but I had no idea how we would get through the end of the month unless God were to provide a miracle. To make matters worse, we had just gotten a resignation letter from our bookkeeper, Marcie, who was not only good at doing our books but had literally been my prayer partner when it came to getting through hard financial months. Marcie felt that our needs had begun to outpace her abilities and that we might be at a point in our organizational growth where we needed an accountant versus a bookkeeper.

I connected with Roger, our board chair, and Brandon Ideker, now the treasurer of the board. They agreed with Marcie that we needed the next level of financial expertise if we were going to continue to grow as an organization. Yet how could I possibly pay the salary level of an accountant when I couldn't even make payroll in two weeks? It was at this juncture that one of my morning Bible verses, Proverbs 24:6, came to mind: "Surely you need guidance to wage war, and victory is won through many advisors."

It certainly felt like a war to me. Everything seemed to be going wrong, and I was in no way equipped to make the decisions that needed to be made . . . and quickly. I had a good, long argument with God and reminded Him that I was really bad at math, had never before owned a business, and hadn't even gone to college. *How am I supposed to know how to handle our finances in the midst of this storm?* At some point in my tirade God reminded me about having an "abundance of counselors."

I had never been called to do this work alone, so I reached out to Tony Scott and Doug Ideker, who agreed to evaluate our finances and our employee structure and make some recommendations. Doug was an experienced business owner and Tony an efficiency expert.

They spent four hours with me and my tiny executive team, which included Amie, Robin, and Katie Cassidy, our development coordinator, in the airless little meeting room in the basement of the house. They asked a lot of questions, helping us to identify our key functions. "What do we absolutely have to have in order to keep offering each program for the girls?" and "Which staff roles are absolutely necessary, and where do we have overlapping roles and responsibilities?"

By the end of the meeting we had identified $200,000 in budget cuts and restructured our staff in a way that would allow us to hire the much needed financial manager with an accounting background. We would have to scrap our plans for leasing new office and GED space, which I could live with. What hurt were the staff cuts. Much as with a school, the vast majority of our budget was in salaries, and there was no way to get to where we needed to be without layoffs and pay cuts.

I left the meeting with my head and my heart waging war against one another. I was proud of our team for not only identifying a path through the current financial calamity but also finding a way to make a key hire in the process. However, I was also filled with dread at having to deliver the news about staff and wage cuts. *How can I ask our loyal team members to take voluntary pay cuts while also letting them know that we will be taking on a new hire?*

I cried the whole way home from work, and I didn't get much sleep that night, desperately framing and reframing the words I would say to each team member. The next morning I woke up exhausted and would have preferred to burrow back under the covers until my kids woke for school, but I dragged myself downstairs for a cup of coffee and a few minutes alone with God.

I twisted open the window blinds to find a gray sky and what looked like a very cold wind blowing through the bare tree in the neighbor's yard. I plopped into the dusty blue armchair I had inherited from my grandma and opened my Bible randomly, trying to quiet my still racing thoughts. Ironically, I had opened to Jeremiah 29:11, the verse painted in pretty, scrolling text above the dining room archway at Hope House: "'For I know the plans I have for you,' says the LORD, 'plans to prosper you and not to harm you. Plans to give you hope and a future.'"

I had always loved this verse for our girls. It was a beautiful reminder to them that God had a plan and a promise for each one of them. But that morning it struck me that God might want me to think about what that verse differently. A thought began to form in my head.

I knew without a doubt that I had reached a crossroads, and I didn't much like it. I could see this beautiful verse as a promise for our teen moms, who held my heart in their sweet hands. Or I could apply this verse to *Hope House* and believe that God meant these words not only for His girls but for the organization as a whole.

God surely had a plan for Hope House, and He was promising a future, despite the crumbling economy. Was I willing to make a huge shift in thinking about my role as being responsible for mamas who had drawn my heart to this work in the first place and instead focus on my responsibility to the *organization*?

As I prayed, something shifted in my heart and mind. In order to best serve our girls, I would have to be willing to make truly difficult decisions about what would be best for the ministry as a whole. In order to not only survive the recession but come out as a stronger organization, I would have to be willing to bear the cost of seeing the organization's future as a promise. This meant letting go of some of my direct responsibilities with the girls and trusting them to the incredible team God had called to Hope House. This was my first realization that leadership is really one long series of learning to let go.

My heart was still heavy when I arrived at Hope House that morning and walked up the painted wooden stairs with the wind whipping tiny crystal snowflakes against my cheeks. However, I also felt a deep sense of resolve. It would become a lifelong effort, but that morning I had taken the first step in releasing my girls to God in order to act on my responsibility to shepherd the organization itself into the future.

I called Alice into my office first. We had hired her as a second GED teacher as that program had grown, and she was good at her job, connecting easily with the girls while also being able to hold them accountable. My next words would impact her life in ways I tried not to imagine. I delivered the difficult message that we had to let one of our GED teachers go and that it was going to be her, based on seniority.

Her eyes instantly filled with tears, and she dropped her head and told me that her husband had just been laid off the night before and that they would be left without an income. As soon as she shared this, I wanted to drag my words back in and tell her she could stay. How could I let her go when she so clearly needed her job? It took everything I had to stay the course, console her for a few minutes, and then usher her out of my office.

I called in Naomi, whom we had just hired as an administrative assistant, and delivered the message that we had to make some really difficult budget decisions. She was shocked at first, but that quickly turned to anger. The questions came: Why hadn't we thought about this messy economy before offering her a job a few weeks earlier? I could only answer with total transparency that her question was completely valid.

When I had hired her, I had been reacting to our need-of-the-moment as administrative tasks had become more demanding. Instead, I should have been carefully planning with an eye to the future and taking into account the current economy, but I wasn't experienced enough to know that. I was sincerely sorry, but I'm not sure that mattered much to her in that moment. I was learning a difficult leadership lesson, and because I hadn't heeded Doug's wise financial advice months earlier, I was learning it at her expense.

From there I moved to a solemn one-on-one meeting with each remaining staff member. Every single one was willing to accept a ten percent reduction in salary, and some were willing to transition to part time. Our staff was united in their commitment to our teen moms and to Hope House, and many of them tried to comfort *me,* knowing how hard the conversation was for me. My heart hurt at having to make layoffs, but it was also full of gratitude for the incredible team of women who were clearly willing to follow the call God was making on their lives, even at a sacrifice.

The last message for me to deliver was to the four teen moms currently living in the House. I knew it would be hard for them to hear about the layoffs, and the last thing I wanted was to create uncertainty for them about the future of their housing. Our entire team gathered in the living room with Angie, Danielle, Megan, and Brittany.

They knew something big was up, as the entire staff had been in and out of my office, and there had been no shortage of tears that day. The girls' faces were tight with worry as they settled into couches and the staff pulled up chairs or sat cross-legged on the floor. Megan's two-year-old son, Tristan, cuddled in her lap, his unruly blonde hair sticking up every which way, as usual. Angie's four-year-old daughter lay on her tummy on the living room rug, coloring in her coloring book, and Danielle's and Brittany's girls were napping.

I was very concerned about allaying their fears. Would they feel unsettled or scared that things were going to fall apart? I know that our moms face a lot of uncertainty and that change is difficult for them. I needed to make sure they were going to be okay as I tried to explain to these teenage moms that people who had worked there weren't going to work there anymore.

"Hope House is facing a tough time right now, and because so many people have lost their jobs and businesses they aren't able to send money to support us as before." I told them that we would *not* let anything happen to the four of them but that we wouldn't be able to take any additional residents at that time. My voice must have cracked a little as I shared this, and Angie immediately scooted forward on the couch.

"I've saved up almost $500 in my cash box in the office," she said. This mama had given our whole staff fits with her stubborn nature and occasional unwillingness to adhere to program requirements. Right now, however, her deep brown eyes were nothing but earnest. "If it will help, I can give my savings to Hope House."

I think every single staff member burst into tears simultaneously. I moved across the room and sat down with Angie, laughing a bit through my tears. I told her that her sweet, generous offer filled all of our hearts with joy but that we had come together as a staff to make sure we could weather this storm and that every single one of us trusted that God would provide what we needed. Nothing was going to happen to their home.

I was drained, to say the least, by the end of that eventful day, but I was also extraordinarily grateful and proud. Every woman on our team had been humbly willing to sacrifice what was needed, and each one had expressed her deep faith in God and her trust in His plan, whatever it might be. These women were living their calling, and nothing could keep them from loving and protecting our girls and their little ones.

My breath fogged the air in my freezing cold car as I quickly climbed in. It was completely dark by now, and the lights shone warmly through the windows of the house as I started my car and cranked the heater. I didn't start driving, though. I just dropped my head and breathed a silent prayer of gratitude. Sometimes prayers don't have—or need—words.

God had called the most amazing women to work at Hope House, surrounding our girls with the kind of stability and love most of them had never before known. I knew without a doubt on that cold February night that I did not, *could not* carry our girls on my own. I could entrust them to the hands of the team members God had called to work at Hope House, which meant that I could focus on building and protecting the ministry as a whole. It wouldn't be easy, but I knew that my job description had changed. I was willing to let go and follow God to wherever He would take me next.

The following week I got a call from Doug. He asked me how I was doing in his strong, deep voice. I told him that I had implemented the decisions we had made as a senior team and thanked him for being so willing to offer his guidance and let me learn from his experience, even when it took me a couple of tries to hear him. He chuckled and reassured me that we would be okay. He also left me with some additional advice:

"Our reaction to our troubles can be a powerful reflection of God's character, if we're willing to let others see it. It isn't easy to share when things are hard, but your champions should know how you're handling this financial crisis, and I urge you to be transparent with where you are at."

I spent the rest of the day making calls to our donors, our champions—not to ask for money but to let them know that we had a plan for weathering the crisis. I was honest in sharing how hard it had been to make those budget cuts, and I also told them that we had asked our prayer team to pray for *them* and for their businesses, as so many of them were having to make difficult choices, just as I was.

Several champions transparently shared their own hard stories of having to close a business or make employee cuts. A few gruff business owners had to clear their throats before responding. All of our champions expressed their gratitude for the call. We were a community, and we would get through this together.

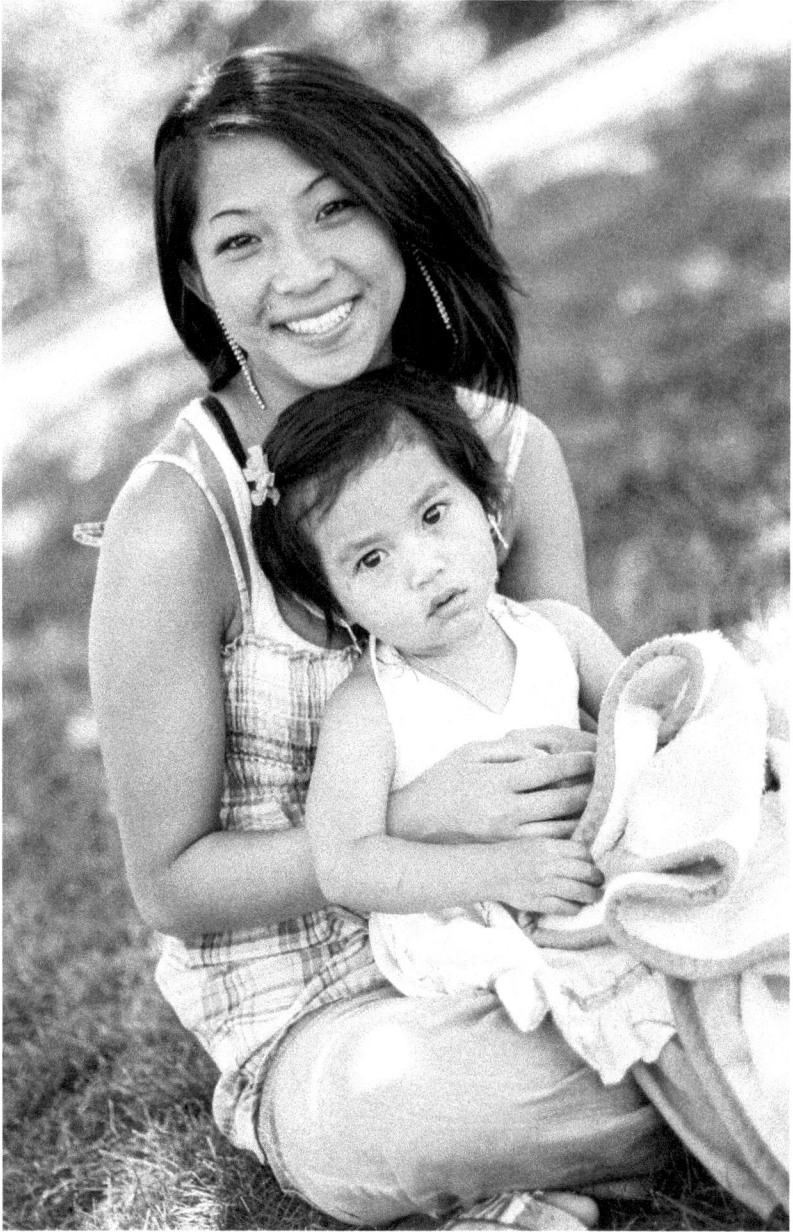

Tina with her daughter, Skarlett, 2009

16

What God Has Provided

Where God guides, God provides.

CHUCK SMITH

Our entire country was dealing with the reality that a broken economy does not impact all people equally. Some nonprofits were closing, faced with a rising demand for their services and a parallel loss of contribution income. People who had been living on the margin before the Great Recession were now being decimated by job loss. Many of those nearing what they had hoped to be the end of their working careers suddenly lost every penny of their retirement accounts. Folks who had never even seen a food bank before were lining up at local food pantries.

Our team at Hope House was dealing with the sad reality that the economic crisis had caused the tension in already stressful households to escalate. Our teen moms were experiencing increased domestic violence, and their parents were increasing drug and alcohol use. Some young moms dropped out of our program altogether, focusing on finding work to help support multigenerational families.

The number of crisis calls from teen moms experiencing homelessness increased dramatically. It tore at our hearts to turn away any teen mom from our residential home, especially when we had empty bedrooms. Yet with only one staff member on duty at any given time, we simply couldn't care for more than the four mamas already living at Hope House. No more money meant no more staff—and frankly, I wasn't sure how we would keep paying the staff we *did* have.

Given the situation, I was pretty shocked when I got a call from our Mentoring Program Manager, Lynn, just as I was arriving at Hope House for the day. Usually cheerful and oozing positivity, this morning her voice sounded a bit frantic. "I just picked up two girls who are on the waiting list for the Mentoring Program. They are sisters, sixteen and eighteen years old. I'm bringing them to the residential house."

My jaw dropped, and I could feel my frustration level rising. Lynn spoke quickly into my shocked silence. "These are the two I've been telling you about, the Vang sisters. They called me this morning from a pay phone and told me they had to sleep in a park last night. Anne's baby, Jacob, was outside all night with them. Tina's baby girl and Anne's older toddler were with their fathers, thank heaven. Tina told me that their mom and stepdad had moved into a new house and taken the youngest sister but refused to let Tina, Anne, and their children come with them. An older sister had said they could stay with her, but last night she kicked them out."

I had been briefed about the two sisters a month earlier and understood that they were in a desperate situation. Their family was Hmong; their mom had emigrated here from Laos and spoke little English. Her first husband was a bitter man, missing everything about his mountainous homeland and often violent with his wife and children. He had abandoned his family when Tina, the youngest, was four years old.

The local Hmong clan leader had arranged a second marriage for Tina and Anne's mom, and additional siblings were born. Unfortunately, the new husband was also abusive, and he became increasingly angry about having to provide for teenaged children he did not consider his own. Matters had worsened when Anne became pregnant, and she was often moving back and forth between older siblings' homes and her mom's house. When Tina also became pregnant at just fourteen, her stepfather refused to allow her to stay in his home. He paid a dowry and arranged for her to marry Joey, the fifteen-year-old father, who was also Hmong.

The convoluted situation seemed incomprehensible to our staff. In doing some research, we learned that a large population of Hmong people had come to the United States in the early 1980s, fleeing the mountains of Cambodia and the genocide unleashed by Pol Pot. Tina and Anne were first-generation Americans, and their parents largely still conformed to historical Hmong cultural norms, with a clan leader carrying legal authority among his people. It didn't matter whether the clan leader's authority was recognized by the state of Colorado, as his people, including the now high school-aged generation born in the United States, still followed this traditional leadership structure religiously.

With permission granted and a ceremony held by the clan leader, Tina was now considered married, and her role in her new household was to clean the home before leaving for school and then to cook the evening meal right after homework. Keeping up with school while completing hours' worth of daily chores became nearly impossible after Skarlett's birth; worse yet, Joey had begun to get violent with Tina during angry outbursts.

A school counselor, unaware of Tina's marriage situation but knowing that she was a new mom, had recommended our Mentoring Program, and Tina had applied and talked Anne into doing the same. Anne was eighteen and had a two-year-old daughter and a second baby boy named Jacob. Jacob's dad was Hispanic, and somehow that was deemed a more serious offense than a teenage pregnancy. Anne's living situation was even more precarious than Tina's.

As I gripped the phone tightly, my mind spun back to the briefing about Tina and Anne's history. I attempted to keep my annoyance with Lynn in check. She was breaking every rule by simply announcing that she was bringing the girls to Hope House, but they were tired, cold, and hungry, and she didn't know what else to do. The truth was that my frustration wasn't aimed at Lynn or at those two poor sisters; it was born out of my fear around our own desperate situation. I knew we would fall in love with those two girls as soon as we saw them, yet we simply didn't have the necessary staff to support them.

As I had foreseen would happen, none of my concerns seemed valid once Lynn brought those two bedraggled girls into the house, one with a baby boy held tightly to her chest, wrapped in the only blanket they had with them. They looked like lost waifs, both of them tiny things with straight black hair falling forward to cover the dark circles under their eyes.

Anne held her baby, Jacob, tightly to her chest, as if still shielding him from the chilly night in the park. Her older daughter and Tina's baby girl had both been with their fathers' families the night before and had escaped having to endure the night under a picnic shelter roof. The two girls looked exhausted, their dark eyes half closed. Lynn ushered them into our huge, light-filled kitchen and quickly whipped up a hot breakfast.

The girls ate hungrily, sitting close to one another at our enormous kitchen table with seating for sixteen. They answered a few of Lynn's quiet questions, but their heads were soon drooping over their scrambled eggs. Our staff got them bundled into twin beds in two of the unoccupied rooms in the twelve-bedroom house.

Once the girls were settled, the staff met to discuss the situation. How could we send them home to such terrible situations? At the same time, it would be irresponsible of us to take them both in when we were short staffed, and we had to consider the girls who already lived in the house, one of whom was giving us a run for our money.

When the sisters awoke from their nap, we sat down with them and talked through the situation. Anne was determined to find a way out of the family drama, and, at eighteen, she was a bit more mature. We determined that we could allow Anne and her children to stay but that Tina would need to move back home to her mother's house.

We would provide her with a mentor immediately and ensure transportation to and from our GED program, hopefully keeping her connected with Hope House while we figured out what to do next. It felt like an inadequate solution, but it was the best we could do at that moment. While the girls had hoped to stay together, they agreed to the temporary solution.

The following Sunday I sat in church with John, still feeling miserable about having sent Tina home but unsure what else we could have done. I had learned the hard way that we couldn't let our hearts get in front of our heads, and best practice was to have two staff on duty at all times. We had been managing with one residential advisor on duty during nonbusiness hours, but this was far from ideal. I was wrestling with my own thoughts and only half listening to our pastor, but somehow a phrase in the sermon snagged my attention: "What are you going to do with what God has already given you?"

I was embarrassed not to even know what the pastor was referencing, but I was suddenly all ears.

"Sometimes we let ourselves get ahead of God," he said. "We assume that, because we are buried in the day to day and God is so far away, we are best equipped to tell Him what our needs are rather than asking Him what He has planned. Well, what if God were to tell us that He simply isn't going to give us *more* right now. What if He were asking us a simple question? *What are you going to do with what I have already given you?*"

That phrase struck my heart, and, frankly, I didn't hear another word of the sermon. I was convicted of the fact that I was thinking about what we *didn't* have at Hope House. "Have you seen the checkbook lately?" was a common refrain for me. But this aha moment was kind of a revelation. *What DO we actually have right now? And why don't I see it?* God knew what we needed to do. He always knows, and His plan is better than our plan.

The next morning I was up early, running the phrase through my mind while staring unseeing at the open Bible in my lap. *Are we being good stewards?* I felt as if the last two months had been a marathon of faithfulness in stewardship, but now I wasn't so sure. I hadn't even stopped to ask the question *What has God already given us?* If I hadn't done so, I certainly couldn't lead my staff to ask it. What if we were to consider this a radical new approach to decision making? How would I even answer the question if I were to stop long enough to think about it?

As soon as I got to work, I pulled my senior team together and told them what I had heard at church. Then I invited them to get creative. "Aside from money, how has God provided during this recession?"

Katie mentioned the prayer request journal she had started. She had already listed three pages of in-kind donations, items our champions had brought in, including a microwave that had shown up almost immediately after our old one had broken. Lynn raised her hand. "Well, we have a flood of new volunteers interested in mentoring."

I chewed on that a moment and then turned to Sue Pilon, our amazing volunteer coordinator, whom the girls called Grandma Sue because she was so tender and loving with everyone she met. "What are you seeing in terms of volunteer interest?"

Sue paused thoughtfully. "We have a lot of new volunteer applications, actually. It seems as if everyone who has lost a job is interested in volunteering their time. Our volunteer hours have been up by about thirty percent month over month.

I sat back in my chair and allowed that to sink in for a moment. I had always assumed that, when I asked God to provide, He would send us money for the things I thought we needed. It also occurred to me that I had never really asked God what *He* thought we needed. An answer started to bubble up inside me, and I blurted out my thoughts: "What if we asked God how He would have us use what He has already provided?"

Blank stares from my team. "Listen, He knows that Anne and Tina need a safe place to call home. He knows that we are short staffed. He has also sent us an abundance of volunteers.

What if we opened ourselves up to the possibility of volunteer staff?"

The response was pretty immediate. "There's no way that could work."

"Volunteers are amazing, but they aren't paid staff—can we rely on them to show up?"

"What about staff meetings?"

"Who is going to want to show up and volunteer to be *actual* staff?"

"All we can do is try," I argued. I felt God saying, *I have already given you the answer. You just haven't looked for it.*

I spent the next several hours reviewing our residential advisor job description and posting it with all of our engaged churches. Inside, I was pretty sure my team was right: Who would ever sign up for this? But it wasn't up to us to decide for the volunteers—only up to us to follow through, put out the opportunities, and then wait to see what was going to happen. But our impulse was to close down the possibility before we'd had a conversation with God. Our impulse was to circumvent the process of volunteering . . . and thus circumvent God's work.

Even as we struggled with the concept, we had several qualified volunteers step forward within the next few weeks, each interested in the role. I explained that we could not pay and that this would be volunteering for the legitimate roles and responsibilities of a staff member, including staff meetings and assigned shifts.

Miraculously, we "hired" and trained four volunteer staff members within a month. One of those volunteers was a college student named Amanda, super energetic with a long blonde ponytail, who came to spend the night at the house every Friday night. What college student wants to do that when she could be out with friends, enjoying her freedom? But Amanda did.

Betty was another volunteer, seventy-five years old with short, dark hair and glasses, perpetually smiling. She had earlier volunteered at an alternative pregnancy center, which meant that she had experience working with teen moms. Both Betty and Amanda would end up as volunteer staff for years: Amanda for two years on those Friday nights and Betty for four years.

Our entire team celebrated when we finally reached double staffing for nonbusiness hour shifts. Lynn got to call Tina to share the news that she and little Skarlett could finally move in. Tina was emotional as her mom signed the intake paperwork and release forms for her to begin participating in the Residential Program. She seemed to be on the verge of tears after her mom left and spent most of the day huddled up with her sister.

I would learn the following day that Tina had spent the weeks following her return home from her brief stay at Hope House banished to the basement of her stepfather's home. She was not welcome there, and he didn't want to see or hear Tina or Skarlett. They had ventured out of the basement only when the stepfather wasn't home and Tina could escape for a few hours to come to GED class. She hadn't told any of us how desperate her situation had become. But God knew. And He had already provided us with exactly what we needed to ensure that both Anne and Tina had a safe place to call home.

I learned a lot from that journey through a national recession, and it would be critical experience a little more than ten years later during an unprecedented global pandemic and economic downturn. For a leader in ministry, it can be tempting to assume that everything we do will be blessed by God. After all, we are doing *His* work.

However, God wasn't going to move our champions to give us more money during those difficult years as I had thought He would. Instead He moved the hearts of a few very committed champions to provide their valuable time, allowing us to literally do the work He had called us into being to do. I am grateful to have learned that God will always provide what we need, though not always in the way that we expect.

Lisa (left) and Amie (right) in their first office in the residential house, 2003

Changing of the Guard

You're braver than you believe,
and stronger than you seem,
and smarter than you think.

AA MILNE

Amie Walton was the kind of person everyone was drawn to. She was funny, charming, quick to laugh, and so smart. Amie was only twenty-three, ten years younger than me, when we started Hope House. She had three energetic kids, the youngest just a baby when we began, yet Amie exuded a boundless amount of energy. She had also been a teen mom, pregnant at nineteen right out of high school, which had put her dreams of nursing school on hold.

She and her then-husband, Tony Walton, were as determined as John and me to bring the Hope House dream to life. Tony was the only one of the four of us to have experienced true generational poverty growing up, and he had an innate understanding of the barriers our moms faced. He also had strong convictions about the choices they needed to make to break the cycle, having joined the army as a teenager to escape the cycle himself.

For the first ten years of our Hope House history, Amie and I worked side by side. In the beginning we were the only full-time staff, and we were a bit like "mom and dad" to the girls. We alternated roles, one of us being the softie and the other holding to the rules and expectations in any given situation with the girls. Our leadership styles sometimes clashed, but we always found a way to resolve issues and work together to push Hope House forward.

By 2009 I had begun to feel a sense of restlessness in Amie. She decided to go back to school part time for a social work degree, believing that this would bring value to our work and at the same time fulfill her longing to learn and grow personally.

For a year she somehow managed to work full time while squeezing in classes, homework, and a busy family life. I shouldn't have been surprised when Amie asked to see me on a gray December morning in 2010. I could tell she was nervous because her knee was bouncing as she sat in the straight-backed, brown, faux-leather chair that I had once thought made my office seem more formal; in reality, it was just uncomfortable.

"Lisa, I have been thinking and praying about this for months, and it is still one of the hardest decisions I have ever made, but I think it's time for me to be done."

I felt my hands go cold, and it seemed as if the air were being sucked right out of the room. Somehow I knew exactly what she meant, while at the same time I found myself unable to process the words. A million thoughts began to instantly swirl in my head. *How will I do this without her? How will the girls feel? What will our champions think?*

I looked into Amie's gold-brown eyes, and she met my gaze directly. I could see that she was nervous and probably sad, but also confident in her decision. I bit my tongue on my immediate reaction to try to talk her out of leaving. I heard the words push past the dryness in my throat without my brain consciously deciding to say them.

"Amie, I don't quite know how I'm going to do this without you as my partner, but I also know that you have dreams and goals beyond this place. I will support you in any way I can. We'll figure this out."

Maybe there was a part of me that had known deep down that Amie and I weren't going to be partners and co-founders forever, but I had never once explored the idea. I felt bereft. I also felt scared. *What if I really can't do this by myself?* I had always had a co-leader, and there was a great deal of comfort in that shared responsibility. It was comforting to have someone to make the big decisions with and to help carry the responsibility for those decisions.

How many nights had I called Amie on my drive home to hash out a problem or celebrate a win? She had been my right arm at work and was one of my best friends outside work. Part of me didn't want to do Hope House without her. There were many nights after that conversation when I would have to pull my car over on the way home because the traffic lights became so blurred by my tears that I couldn't safely drive.

In the following days Amie and I talked in depth about how to best communicate her decision. One of the wisest things we ever did was to hire a consultant to build a transition plan around Amie's departure. We had never paid a consultant to work with us before, but we knew we had to invest in outside expertise to guide us through this time.

It was important that our staff and champions didn't view Amie's departure as a "break up" and lose confidence in the ministry. It was also critical to me that we honor Amie's work and preserve the most important aspects of what she had brought to Hope House every day. With the consultant's guidance and the feedback of staff and teen moms, we developed our first culture statement. What Amie brought to our teen moms from her very first day until her last was an unrelenting positivity, a sense of humor, and a feeling that there was always room for fun.

We cemented Amie's legacy into the final sentence of our culture statement: "At Hope House we find a little bit of silliness in every day." It was as if God put His stamp of approval on the statement when we emerged from our conference room with the consultant to find that the staff had started a silly string fight with the girls while we worked. Staff and teen moms stood in the living room covered in colorful, rubbery strands of string, which also dripped off furniture and covered the floor. There was a moment of guilty silence, and then Amie burst out laughing; even the consultant couldn't help but join in.

To this day the picture we took of silly, string-covered staff graces the pages of our HR Manual right underneath the culture statement. Amie will forever bring her sense of joy and fun to teen moms across the country as more Hope House homes open and adopt the culture statement written that day.

Ultimately, a decision had to be made about who would move into Amie's role as Program Director. After a lot of prayer and consultation with our board chair, I offered the position to Robin Scott. Robin had been an amazing Residential Program Manager, calm, steady and wise. She was never ruffled when the girls were acting out and balanced grace and truth as no one else.

She knew how to love our moms unconditionally and generously, even when they weren't acting very lovable. She also knew when to say no and hold to the boundaries. Her decisions were fair but final, and the girls trusted her.

As soon as Robin had accepted the role, I began making phone calls. Our consultant had helped us develop a communication plan and talking points for sharing the news. It was important that our champions feel that we still had solid, stable leadership in place, as it is not uncommon in major transitions for donors to feel as if they should pull back their giving until they see how things are going to shake out. We were definitely not in a financial position to start losing champions, as we were still recovering from the Great Recession and had little money in savings.

I started by calling my most trusted advisors, Christine Bess, Doug Ideker, and John Scott. None of them seemed as surprised or concerned as I had expected. In fact, they were all briefly sympathetic but supportive, reassuring me of my ability to lead Hope House through the transition and appreciative of being informed in person. Feeling a bit relieved, I called every one of our most engaged volunteers and donors, sharing the news and our plan to transition Robin into the role.

Everyone was excited for Amie, and the few who expressed concern, mainly for the impact on the girls, seemed relieved by the choice of Robin Scott as a successor. As a final step, we sent out a letter with Amie's farewell note and my update on the transition plan. During that time I learned how true it is that communication is key. It is critical to make sure that everyone impacted by big events or major transitions feels informed and has the chance to ask questions and process the change.

No longer having a co-leader brought a certain amount of freedom and nimbleness to decision making, but it was also a lonely place. So, it came as a blow when only one year later Robin also chose to leave Hope House, as she and Tony had decided to open a business together.

After much consideration and prayer, I offered Nicole Feltes the role of Program Director after Robin had stepped down. Nicole had held various program positions, including Residential Manager, and I knew how bright and talented she was. Nicole was relatable, creative, and funny, and the girls loved her. She made everyone laugh with her offbeat remarks, and someone even hung a whiteboard just for capturing Nicole-isms. She had a knack for making complex things simple, and without her we never would have developed our self-sufficiency measurement system.

Self-sufficiency is complex, covering every area of life, and for our teen moms it has to be viewed through the lens of generational poverty, with a focus on how to empower our moms to break unhealthy and destructive family cycles. For many years we had loosely based our work on Ruby Payne's *Bridges Out of Poverty*, which provides a framework for understanding the dynamics that perpetuate poverty, from the individual to the systemic level.

Each class system, from poverty to middle class to wealth, has a set of hidden rules around values, resources, family structure, language, and more, which are critical to understand if attempting to move from one class system to another (consider the number of people who win the lottery but go on to lose all of the money within a few short years, as they have no idea how to navigate the hidden rules of the wealth class).

All of the institutional systems in our country are built on middle class values, from schools to hospitals to banking. Even our human services systems are designed to support those in poverty . . . but not to empower them to break *out* of poverty. It is incredibly challenging for our teen moms to break the cycle of generational poverty, and it is our job to build on their intrinsic strength and determined mommy motivation to empower them with the knowledge, tools, and relationships to do so.

When Hope House first opened, we used a simple goal-setting process, allowing our moms to identify where they wanted to go and helping them craft goals to get there. As we grew, we knew we needed a more complex way to measure the results, not just for individual teen moms but for the organization as a whole. Through the years I had participated in workshops on process evaluation, outcome evaluation, logic models, and more. I had learned about qualitative versus quantitative measurement and believed the adage that "what gets measured gets done."

However, data and measurement were certainly not my first language, so when it became clear that we had to upgrade the way we measured the girls' progress, I asked Nicole to take the lead on the project. With her help and the guidance of an old friend, Monica Geist, who held a PhD in Quantitative & Qualitative Analysis, we began a one-year project to build a rubric that would actually measure self-sufficiency growth.

At my first meeting with Monica in a local restaurant, she drew up a simple rubric right there on the paper tablecloth, which I subsequently ripped off and stuffed in my purse. For months afterward we would pin that piece of tablecloth to the wall during every work session.

Under Nicole's leadership we eventually landed on a rubric that measures self-sufficiency in six economic domains and nine personal domains. With this system in place, our Community

Program Manager, Jenny Macias, finally felt that she had gained some traction in moving our moms forward.

When Nicole made the decision to move back to St. Louis to be near family, it was an easy decision for me to move Jenny into the role of Program Director. Jenny is a vivacious leader with a seemingly endless amount of positivity and an incredibly deep love and respect for our teen moms. By this time I had finally begun to understand how fluid our staffing structure would likely always be. Looking back, I can see that there were in some sense generations of teams, each one exactly what we needed for each stage of our organizational development.

I count it a bonus blessing that I have gotten to know and love so many Hope House team members throughout the years. I have gotten to see deep and lasting friendships form between many of them. Katie and Elizabeth are two names always spoken in the same sentence even today.

Katie held various roles at Hope House, from fundraising to program, and she formed an immediate attachment to Elizabeth, our first GED Coordinator. When Elizabeth was diagnosed with stage 4 ovarian cancer at just twenty-nine years old, Katie was her champion. She pushed for Hope House to begin offering health insurance, even though I wasn't sure we could afford to, because at the time a person with a pre-existing condition could be insured only under a group healthcare plan. Today Elizabeth has been cancer free for a decade, and she and Katie are still best friends, while various other team members are still roommates and book club buddies or have been bridesmaids in one another's weddings.

It is true that change is a constant in our ministry, just as it is in life. However, change can be hard, and our staff and teen moms are rocked every time a leader or team member decides to move on. My own innate reaction to change is to put down my head and plow forward. This, however, is most definitely *not* helpful to my team. Robin once gave me a piece of wise advice that I rely on to this day: "You're the leader. Everyone needs to hear *you* say that it's going to be okay."

Being the leader requires me to be the encourager, even when I least feel like it. I can indulge in a private pity party over a glass of wine on my back deck, but publicly I must demonstrate to others that I have my eyes fixed on our unchanging Leader and that I truly trust that He is in the midst of the change.

From left to right: Mindy, Lisa, Christine, John, and Lisa signing the land deal, 2015

18

You Must Be Out of Your Flippin' Tree

Start by doing what's necessary;
then do what's possible;
and suddenly you are doing the impossible.

FRANCIS OF ASSISI

L isa Schlarbaum joined our board of directors after having donated a toddler bed that her son, Max, had outgrown. She had heard about us through her church and came for a tour of the house. She was drawn to the ministry because her mother-in-law had been a teen mom and because of her strong belief in education, as she had watched her own grandparents break the cycle of poverty through education.

Lisa was in sales for a large paper corporation. She brought to the board a level of energy and a sense of urgency that we hadn't previously had. A formidable leader, Lisa never met a challenge she couldn't overcome or a goal she couldn't achieve.

I often joke that it took me three years to talk her off our board (and out of her big sales salary) and onto our small staff. In truth, the decision to become our Director of Development came at no small cost to Lisa and her family. She had worked her way up the corporate ladder and had planned to retire early. Accepting a call to come and help grow our small ministry was a huge change of plans, and Lisa is nothing if not a planner.

I found out years later that Lisa told God that she would give this calling three years and then go back to the corporate world. More than a dozen years later, she is still making huge things happen at Hope House and is nowhere near retirement.

I'll never forget my first meeting with Schlarbie, as our staff came to call her to differentiate between the two Lisas. We were in the little classroom in the basement of the house, and Lisa was at the whiteboard, marker in hand. Lisa asked hard questions and expected me to have answers.

We had been over the annual budget, which was around $800,000 at the time. I had covered our fundraising strategies, including the golf tournament and annual gala, the direct appeal letters, and grants from local foundations. Still, Lisa's agitation was clear. She flipped her long blonde curls over one shoulder and started drawing on the whiteboard.

"Look, you've identified exactly how much the events and letters and grants are bringing in," she said, jotting numbers on the board in her crooked handwriting. "But this is only about half of your income. Where does the other $400,000 a year come from?"

"I guess I don't really know," I responded. "Honestly, it's as if God provides, and we seem to always have just enough for our needs."

"So, half your income is God-money?" she asked incredulously. "How am I supposed to replicate that? It isn't exactly a strategy!" Schlarbie drew a long line on the board with a big funnel on the end. "You have to know what's in the pipeline." She gestured to the line. "You have to know what's coming into the funnel."

I was a little bit out of my depth with her, but in a good way. I listened carefully as Lisa started analyzing trends, setting goals, and defining strategies for reaching them. This wasn't unlike what we ask of our mamas: identify where you want to be in three years, understand the obstacles, and build an action plan to get there.

Schlarbie had a gift for translating her sales background into development or fundraising, but more than that, she had a heart for transformational giving. She was fascinated by the concept we had adopted a few years earlier after having attended a workshop led by the Mission Increase Foundation, or MIF. MIF offers free biblical fundraising training, teaching ministries on how to ensure that our donors, or champions, will experience God through their giving.

I loved the way transformational giving aligned with the way we felt about our champions. Our love for them was second only to our love for the girls and their little ones. Lisa grabbed onto the concept and operationalized it, something I hadn't even known we needed to do. Schlarbie is smart, determined, and a master at motivating people. Looking back, I can see God's timing in bringing this amazing woman to Hope House. He was about to lead us into the next big phase of our journey, and we were going to need Lisa Schlarbaum to get there.

In late 2011 the church next door decided to sell the land they owned to the south of our residential home. I would sometimes sit in my office and gaze out the window at the big red, white, and blue "for sale" sign in the middle of the overgrown field where our house had once sat while waiting to be moved onto its foundation. I recalled the way Robin Scott would sometimes stand on our front porch and stare across the field in the same manner I now was. Even then she was sure that the land was meant for us and that we were supposed to build a Resource Center on it for our mamas.

Our Mentoring and GED Programs were growing, and we had opened our residential, parenting, and healthy relationship classes to our community moms, as we now called them. We were now serving around forty girls a year. We had only two small rooms in the church next door, and while the church had allowed us to paint and decorate the rooms it was still the church, and it just didn't *feel* the same as when you walked into the house. Still, the thought of buying the land and building a place for our teen moms seemed too far out of our reach to be a real possibility . . . until the day Brian Bess came to see me.

Brian's wife, Christine, was a former board member and had become a good friend. We were both part of a Bible study that Tami Bandimere hosted at her family's famous NHRA racetrack, Bandimere Speedway. That group of ladies was and is my life group, always encouraging me but also willing to hold me accountable to my faith and my calling.

Christine was a learner, super smart and always willing to ask the tough questions. She might have been intimidating if I hadn't known how much her heart beat for Hope House and our mamas. When she called me one morning to say that her husband, Brian, was going to drop by Hope House, I was surprised. Brian was an engineer who worked in oil and gas. Like Christine, he was analytical and smart and always asked good questions. He hadn't been to the house in a few years, since having helped with the demolition after we had moved it.

Brian's visit was brief. We sat in my office, and he asked how things were going with the girls. Then he asked how things were going financially. I was always nervous when someone asked hard financial questions. We had moved to accrual accounting versus operating on a cash basis, under the leadership of our Finance Director Tena Thwaites. With Schlarbie bringing in more dollars and Tena helping us grow strategically, we were in a better financial position than ever before.

Yet I still had trouble understanding the monthly financials without poring over them prior to a meeting. I felt as if I fumbled the answers to Brian's questions, and he left without telling me why he had wanted to visit. I was puzzled but figured that maybe he had wanted to check on his investment, since he and Christine gave about $10,000 a year, which was no small amount.

Two weeks later Brian's visit had fled my mind . . . until Christine and I were walking to our cars together after Bible study one cold February morning. My breath was clouding the air, and I wasn't wearing a coat, but Christine wanted to chat for a few minutes.

"So, I want to talk to you about something Brian and I have been discussing around Hope House."

"Sure, what have you guys been talking about?"

Without preamble Christine made a statement my brain couldn't quite compute: "Brian wants to give you the money to buy the land." I just stared at her, not quite processing, as I was pretty sure they couldn't afford to do something like that.

"What do you mean?" I asked, stomping my feet a bit in the snowy parking lot, trying to warm my toes.

"Brian sold a business, and we're putting the funds into a family foundation, and we want to buy the land the church is selling so that you can build the Resource Center."

My brain was as foggy as the air when I spoke. "Wait, what business? I didn't even know Brian owned a business!"

"Lisa, we are donating the $215,000 you need to buy that land," she said with a small laugh and a shake of her short blonde hair.

"Oh my gosh! You're doing *what*?" It finally hit me that she was serious, and I grabbed her arms and started jumping up and down and shouting and laughing all at the same time. Christine just laughed with me, and after a few minutes she said, "Well, I guess you'll have to start thinking about a capital campaign to raise the money to build a building on that land." I was so excited that just about anything seemed possible, even though I had no idea how to conduct a capital campaign.

A week later I was sharing the amazing news with our board of directors at our monthly meeting. I was beyond excited, and it didn't even occur to me that the board might not feel the same way. As a leader I was learning that you need other leaders around you to bring you back to reality, to keep you from rushing pell mell ahead. I have a tendency to get ahead of God, and I needed cooler heads to help me work through the implications of the gift.

Our then-Chair, Mindy Brown, quieted the room and began asking questions about our financial position and our capacity to even do a feasibility study, which was the first step in a capital campaign and would require hiring a consultant to meet with our champions to determine whether they would commit to something like this. Our former Chair, Stacy Hougland, asked the question everyone seemed to be afraid to ask: "Should we even accept the gift?"

Suddenly everyone seemed to be talking at once. My heart was in my throat. I wanted so badly to convince everyone that this was the next step. This was what our moms needed. This would be their place to belong, not two small rooms in a church but their very own space.

Yet Stacy and Mindy were two strong leaders and women I respected greatly. I knew they wanted to make the right and best decision for the ministry as a whole. The meeting ended with no conclusion to the discussion. We all agreed to spend the month praying and asking God for guidance in what was honestly the biggest decision we would most likely ever make.

My husband, John, had been quiet during the board meeting, but a week later he came home from work with a whole lot to say. He was visibly impatient as he paced our small kitchen.

"We need to take that gift. I think this is a God-thing. I keep hearing Pastor Tellis in my head. We have to look back and see where God has shown up for us in the past. This is another one of those 'You're out of your flippin' tree moments.' God is about to do something that we can't do on our own, which is what makes it a God thing!"

John was convicted enough to write the board a long email, which, if you don't know my husband, is saying something. His words are almost always brief but impactful, and his emails are seldom longer than two sentences. That night he wrote two pages, reminding the board that God had called a group of people with no resources, no background in nonprofits, and no connections to open a home for teen moms.

He reminded them of the words of a realtor we had met with long ago, when we had first begun exploring the idea of Hope House. The man had warned us that we would never find rent under $1,500, that the neighbors would complain, and that the zoning would be a challenge. In the end he had told our fledgling board that we were 'out of our flippin' trees.'"

John's email reminded the board of how, despite the challenges, God had led us to a huge house with no neighbors and a $350 rent payment. Then, when the house was slated to be torn down, God had led the organization that owned the home to donate it to us, and the church to donate land to put it on.

John concluded the email with a reminder of Pastor Tellis's words: "We have to be aware of how God has worked in Hope House in the past and stay mindful of that. God led the Bess family to provide for the land. I believe that God *wants* it to look like we are out of our flippin' trees because then it will be clear to the whole world that *He* is doing this."

With that reminder every single board member voted to accept the gift from the Bess family and move forward with the vision to build a Resource Center for our teen moms. As we often did after board meetings, John and I went out to dinner to debrief and relax. After that meeting we sat at the restaurant staring into each other's eyes with a feeling of awe. "I can't believe what God is doing, that we get to be a part of this, and that this is our story." I was overcome with a feeling of deep gratitude that we were getting to do it together. We were going to build a building!

Mindy Brown helped me draft a "request for" proposal, which would go out to potential consultants for the feasibility study. Schlarbie, who had no more experience with a capital campaign than I did, wasn't intimidated one bit. She set out to find a mentor who could guide her through the structure, timeline, marketing, and logistics of a capital campaign. I began a series of meetings with the city around the rezoning process. I figured we would have a groundswell of support, just as we'd had when we moved the house.

Instead, we began running into significant roadblocks and challenges. We had chosen a consulting firm to conduct our feasibility study at a cost of over $10,000, which we could barely afford at the time. Our consultant, Scott, was a professorial looking man with tufts of gray hair and wire rimmed glasses who didn't mince words. He made sure we understood that his job was to objectively assess our ability and capacity to raise the kind of money it would take to build this Resource Center. He would be meeting with our donors one-on-one, without Lisa or me in attendance, allowing them to speak freely about their thoughts on the project and their willingness to contribute to it.

When I reached out to Carol Ibanez, the city planner we had worked with when the house was donated, I learned that there would be no miracle zoning match for this project. The land would have to be rezoned to a multipurpose zone in order to accommodate our desired use. This would require having a preliminary development plan—a fancy way of saying that the city needed to know almost exactly what we planned to do with the land before we could rezone it. We would have to have architectural plans, landscape plans, civil plans, and structural plans—essentially, we would have to design the entire project *before we even knew if we would get the rezoning!*

In order to buy the land, we had to know that it could be rezoned for our proposed use, or we would be wasting the Bess's gift. Yet we couldn't get a rezoning without completing extensive plans that we had no money to pay for. This was like driving into a traffic circle with no clear direction and no way out.

The "temporary" resource center in Westminster, 2012

19

Another Unexpected Move

*The Promised Land always lies
on the other side of a wilderness.*

HAVELOCK ELLIS

O nce again I turned to the amazing people God had surrounded us with. One gentleman named Bill Maul was a new Hope House champion. Bill developed luxury homes, and I knew he could provide some guidance on where to even start with the design of a building. After we had moved the house, it had gone through an extensive remodel. This new challenge would be entirely different, with a 15,000-square-foot building that needed to be designed from the ground up. Bill quickly introduced me to Jeanne Fielding, an architect he often worked with. Jeanne was willing to do our initial design work for free, a miracle in and of itself.

Next, I reached out to Bryon White, owner of Milender White Construction, a large company in Denver. Bryon's own mother had been a teen mom, and he had become a regular donor after having made a gift in his mom's honor one year. Soon we had a small building committee formed.

I began asking for donations for the preliminary development plan. One of the most significant pieces would be the civil engineering. I reached out to Jeff French at Peak Civil, and, miraculously, he was moved to help and committed to doing the civil engineering for free. I had also recently met Karla Nugent, who had co-founded Weifield Electrical Group, a large electrical contracting company in Denver.

Karla had introduced me to a group of women in the construction industry called the Kick-Ass Women's Leadership Group, or KAWLG. Karla had invited me to speak to their group several months earlier, and since that time this group of high-powered women in the building industry have taken me under their wing. One member of the group owned a landscape architecture firm, and she volunteered to draft the landscape plans free of charge!

Things seemed to be falling into place with our preliminary development plan on the design side. However, moving through the city process was more difficult. We had to present our ideas, followed by preliminary plans, to the planning department, followed by a formal presentation to the planning commission, who would then make a recommendation to city council, where we would present once again for a final decision.

A part of this process required us to host a neighborhood meeting. The city provided the names and addresses of the neighbors within a one-mile radius of Hope House, and we sent out a letter sharing all about our amazing teen moms and their need for a space to learn and grow. We invited them to the neighborhood meeting, to be held in the gym of the church.

Representatives of the city would be present, as well as our architect, Jeanne Fielding, and most of our board, and our letter stated that we would be happy to answer any questions the neighbors might have. I happily remembered how, after our house move and subsequent request for a special use permit for our residential home, the neighbors had gathered with us outside city council chambers, excited to volunteer at Hope House.

The evening of the meeting was cool and clear, and the bright white steeple of the church stood in stark contrast to the dark blue evening sky. The scent of the freshly mown church lawn filled the air. Inside the church gym we set out rows of folding chairs and a table with a big display of our proposed project, including amazing elevations that Jeanne had drawn up. We'd had them blown up in color so everyone could see how beautiful our new building would be. We created lists of answers to the concerns we thought would be most pressing.

I felt confidant and excited to share our plans . . . at least until the first neighbors began filing in. There were about two dozen people, and most of them seemed angry. They filled their seats and sat with their arms crossed and frowns on their faces, ignoring the cookies and coffee we had set out.

Everyone was respectful during the presentation, and no one interrupted us as we shared about the girls we serve and how much they needed a safe and loving place to learn; grow; and build relationships with staff, volunteers, and one another. I thought I had done a pretty good job of sharing the "why," and Jeanne did a great job of sharing the design and how the facility would fit into the surrounding neighborhood. However, as soon as we were done talking, the hands started flying in the air.

One neighbor was angry that we would displace a family of foxes that lived in the field.

Another demanded, "How are you going to guarantee my property value won't go down?"

Another objected, "We don't like the plans for the playground. It will be too loud!"

The tension in the air began to build as each neighbor had a turn to speak. The city staff were taking notes, and so was I. Finally, the microphone passed to Dean, a man who lived directly behind Hope House. My palms started to sweat a little. I knew that Dean didn't like us. He had made a few hostile phone calls over the years, usually swearing at me and accusing one of our residents of something he didn't like, such as smoking and throwing cigarette butts in his yard (which to my knowledge had never once happened).

Dean was tall and stocky, probably in his mid-fifties, and he stood with his legs planted, his feet in giant work boots. He stared directly at me. "Look lady, you need to understand one thing. We don't want your warehouse full of unwanted kids in our backyard."

My mouth literally dropped open. You could have heard a pin drop as the neighbors suddenly quieted, quickly followed by murmured notes of dissent. "We didn't say *that,* exactly!"

I was furious. What an unbelievable comment, fueled by ignorance. *You are displaying the exact type of horrible judgment on these girls and their children that causes there to be a need for Hope House in the first place!*

Carol Ibanez sensed that I was fuming and quickly stood and took the mic, redirecting the conversation to previously articulated questions. She shared city code requirements around traffic and parking lot lights, addressing some concerns quickly.

She let the neighbors know we would address additional concerns before the planning commission meeting and invited everyone to attend that if they still had issues.

Dean wasn't satisfied and stood abruptly, as if he had something further to say, but ultimately he just turned and stomped out of the gym. The rest of the neighbors began filing out, some forming tight knots in the church parking lot, murmuring to one another.

Our staff and board were pretty stunned by the tension at the meeting, especially Dean's vicious comment. As we gathered our displays and picked up the uneaten cookies, my shock began turning to anger. How dare he talk about our mamas and children that way? Thank goodness none of our girls had been in attendance, or I would have been tempted to beat the man over the head with the microphone!

The next morning I pulled into the driveway of the house and sat staring at the large, particle-board sign that we were required to stake in the field, announcing the planned use for the property. I felt discouraged and angry at the same time. Deflated.

This was so opposite the way the neighbors had reacted when we'd built the house. There had been positivity and acceptance. Now those warm and fuzzy responses appeared to be gone. I didn't think the morning could get much worse . . . until I walked into my office to find the phone ringing. I snatched it up and answered, hoping my voice sounded more polite than I felt.

"Hi, Lisa, it's Carol Ibanez. We need to discuss the meeting last night." I was sure that she wanted to discuss how rude the neighbors had been and to coach me on how to handle the upcoming planning commission meeting.

"One of the neighbors mentioned that there are a lot of people in and out of the house each day. Why is that?"

Surprised at the question, I responded that we had more staff now, as we were operating our GED Program and Mentoring Program and had a new counselor who was designing healthy relationship classes for the girls.

"Well," Carol answered slowly, "you can't really do all of that out of the house. You have a residential special use permit. You are allowed only to use the house for residential programming."

Stunned, I sat back in my chair. She was right. How could I have forgotten that we had a residential group home permit? Our ministry had grown so organically, simply meeting the needs of more girls and meeting them where they were at, that it hadn't occurred to me that we had grown beyond the initial permitting for our home.

Carol went on to say that the city would allow us time to find a place to go but that everything that wasn't residential would have to be moved out of the house. I felt a sense of déjà vu, as if no time had passed and David Nestor had just called to say that we would have to find another place to go because they were going to tear down the house.

"How much time do we have?"

"Typically, the city would expect you to become compliant within two weeks. However, we can give you a month if that would help."

I almost laughed but quickly squelched the impulse and thanked Carol for the grace period. A month! *That's impossible!* How would we find a place to rent—and even if we could, how would we afford it? I dropped my head onto the desk and just prayed. *What would You have us do, God? And how can I possibly break my staff and moms in half and take half of them to another location?* The thought nearly broke my heart.

When I called my staff together to share the news, they were just as unhappy as I was. Our team absolutely loved being in the house, interacting with the residents and their kids every single day. As we talked it through, an idea began to emerge. I figured we needed only about a year to complete our building project, and then we would all be together in our new building. What if we just borrowed more space at the church? Everyone loved the idea, and I quickly placed a call to the pastor.

The church was excited at the prospect of coming alongside us in such a significant manner yet again. Two weeks passed in a blur as we made plans for what additional space in the church we could use. The logistics became more complicated, however, as we started navigating the need to schedule our programs around the church activities. But things came to a screeching halt the day I called the power company to ask about additional power to support all of our computers at the church.

It was an old building, and they were already using most of what the electrical load allowed. In order to support our needs, we would have to add a new transformer to the building, a cost that could be well over $10,000. We didn't even have $5,000 in our savings account. We had hit a dead end. Again.

Discouraged, I sent an email to the board, informing them of the news. I also emailed the prayer team and asked them to start praying, because I had no idea how we were going to fix this. God, however, wasn't at a loss. Within two days I received an email from Laurie Scott. She had read the prayer request and reached out to her friend David Johnson, whose company owned half the warehouse space in town. David was willing to let us use one of his spaces rent free! He offered us a 2,200-square-foot space in Westminster, about ten minutes north of Hope House.

The irony that we would be operating out of a warehouse was not lost on me, and, frankly, it was unsettling the first time I visited the building. It sat in a row of identical one-story white concrete buildings. There was a tiny vestibule, which led to a hallway that had a narrow counter on one side with a tiny sink and a microwave beneath a row of cabinets.

The hallway opened directly into the warehouse, which had a tall ceiling, cement floors, and drywall only halfway up the walls, with the rest just exposed insulation. On the back wall was a huge garage door for loading trucks. As generous as the offer was, this space didn't seem very Hope-Housey.

Still, it seemed pretty miraculous that we had been offered space so quickly, and practically for free. Plus, the City of Westminster considered our use "educational" and allowed the use in industrial space. With the help of one of our volunteers, Sharon, whom we called our magical-wonderful-space planner, we began to see a vision develop for the space.

Even if we were going to be there for only a year, it would have to be habitable. Sharon arranged for the donation of office furniture from a local credit union, and Lundquist Associates offered to drywall over the garage door to keep out the freezing winter air, as well as to cover the exposed insulation and painting for us.

We secured a donation of carpet squares and covered the cement floor. David Johnson even offered to install a large cooling unit, as the space was heated but not cooled and we would be miserable in the hot summer months without cool air. By the time we were ready to move in, the space felt much more inviting.

The makeover, however, did little to lift the spirits of our staff, all of whom, including me, felt disconnected from the house and the residents. There was no longer a constant stream of children toddling into our office space, or teen moms coming in to plop down and talk.

Finally, at our first all-staff meeting in the new space, Lisa Schlarbaum had had enough. We had rolled our chairs into a circle in the middle of the desks that now lined the walls. After opening in prayer, Lisa began to talk, her voice gaining in intensity with each word she spoke.

"Listen, everyone, we cannot have this! God has given us a huge opportunity here! We should be excited and grateful! God does not just live at the House! God lives wherever He has chosen for His girls to be! Now everyone, lift your right hand in the air."

The energy in the room had definitively shifted. Lisa was a powerful motivator, and as she was speaking I could see the staff straightening in their chairs and the smiles returning to their faces. We all waited eagerly, hands in the air, and I was sure she was about to tell us to high five one another. Instead, with a toss of her blonde curls, she half shouted, "Now turn to the person next to you and give her a slap and tell her to snap out of it!"

With that she turned and lightly slapped Jenny Macias on the cheek. Jenny's mouth dropped, and every other hand stayed frozen in the air until someone started to giggle. Then someone else broke into full laughter, and within seconds the whole room was howling.

The story of Lisa slapping Jenny has become legendary and is passed down to new generations of staff to this day whenever some change feels big and scary. Change is hard. That big move was going to change our DNA, and we sensed that. But if we hadn't opened ourselves up to God doing a new thing, we would have missed the many miracles He still had in store for Hope House and our girls.

Janelle with her sons, Jacob (left) and Joseph (right), 2016

20

Muddy Poster Child

Even if you're on the right track,
you'll get run over if you just sit there.

WILL ROGERS

s I was driving to work one morning a new song came on the radio. It was a pretty tune, and I hummed along with the chorus: "Settle down, don't let the fear drag you down, I'm gonna make this place your home." I broke into a wide smile, feeling as if God had spoken straight to my heart. He *had* made our new mini-Resource Center feel like home within a short time.

We had lots of new teen moms coming in for GED tutoring at the three folding tables in the center of our one big room, surrounded by a ring of staff desks. Ashley Palacios was our newest GED Coordinator, and she was a master at moving the girls through the GED. She was passionate about alternative education paths and had started championing the idea of moving our girls beyond GED and on to college. One mom in particular pulled at Ashley's heart, and mine.

Janelle was a quiet girl and very private about her life outside Hope House. She had a three-year-old son, Joseph, and a baby boy named Jacob. We would later learn that Janelle and her mom had frequented domestic violence shelters often during her childhood. She had gotten pregnant at fifteen and had ended up moving to Denver with her boyfriend, but his abuse finally forced her to leave, and she had ended up sleeping on the streets with Joseph for a short time.

Then she met someone who seemed to care deeply for her, and, after getting pregnant a second time, she moved in with him and his parents. The situation was not stable, however, as the boyfriend's mom didn't like Janelle at all.

One night late in the evening my cell phone rang. I didn't typically pick up after business hours, but for some reason I answered. Janelle's voice was panicked, and I had to ask her to slow down and take a deep breath. Shakily, she did so, and then proceeded to tell me that she had been kicked out of the house with both boys. She was in her car, but she was almost out of gas. A winter storm watch had been issued, and she was terrified that she wouldn't be able to keep the car running and the heat on. She wanted to know if I could please help her get gas.

My heart was breaking for her. She was a very proud young woman, a strong person who never wanted to ask for help, but at this point she didn't know what else to do. When our teen moms ask for help, we have to hold those pleas with honor and tenderness. Yet, it is also important we don't just rescue our girls; we want to empower them, and there is a fine line between empowering and enabling. In this case Janelle needed rescue, and quickly. There was no way she would be sleeping in her car with an expected ten inches of snow on the way.

Fat flakes were already sticking to the roads, driven by fierce winds, as I pulled into the parking lot of the hotel where I had instructed her to meet me. I had picked up McDonalds meals for Janelle and the kids on the way over, and as she settled Joseph on the hotel bed with his Happy Meal she turned to me with wide brown eyes full of tears.

"Why are you doing this for us?" she asked, her voice quavering. Then she launched herself into my arms and hugged me. I swallowed around the lump in my throat and smoothed back a strand of brown hair that had escaped from her ponytail.

"Janelle, this is what Hope House is here for. We love you and your kids, and we want more than anything else for you to be safe. You and the boys get a good night's sleep, and tomorrow we'll see about getting you an interview for the Residential Program." Fortunately, we had an opening, and Janelle and her boys moved in the following day.

While the program staff was handling a growing number of teen moms, Schlarbie was busy spearheading our feasibility study and chomping at the bit for results so that we could begin fundraising in earnest for our new building. Finally, we got the call from Scott, our consultant. He had met with our champions and was ready to present his report to our board. Lisa and I could hardly stand the anticipation. We knew that our champions loved us and were sure the results would be exactly what we wanted to hear.

We couldn't have been more wrong. Scott looked serious as he passed the bound copies of the feasibility report around the table at our borrowed meeting room on the campus of a local college. He began to speak in his professorial manner, first sharing that the champions he had met with did, indeed, love both Hope House and our teen moms. They loved that the Residential Program allowed our moms a safe place to live and the way the GED Program successfully helped them finish school. However, the Mentoring Program confused them.

"The truth is, you've got yourself a muddy poster child. Your champions think your moms will be just fine if they have a place to live at the residential home, or if they just get their GED through your GED Program and get a job. They don't understand why your teen moms need a mentoring program— or a big building. In fact, it is my professional opinion that you will do well to raise $750,000. It is very unlikely that you will be able to raise the $3.5 million you're projected to need in order to build your Resource Center."

You could have heard a pin drop in the room as the board sat in collective disbelief. Then the questions began to fly. At first the board seemed defensive, quickly followed by a sense of group concern. Ultimately, we left the board meeting with Mindy wisely urging us to take time to process the results of the feasibility study and not to jump to any quick decisions or conclusions. Personally, I hadn't even gotten past the defensive stage when we left the meeting.

Muddy poster child indeed. *What does that even mean?*

Ultimately, Lisa and I discovered that our champions didn't understand the barriers our teen moms faced in their journey to self-sufficiency. We had never communicated to our champions the complexities of generational poverty or the generational trauma our girls had experienced.

As I made my way through the fifty-page report, I realized that what we actually had in that feasibility study was a roadmap to success! I began making notes, stopping to process every point of concern. I detailed a potential response to as many of these as I could, ending up with eleven pages of notes.

Next, Schlarbie and I sat down with our Communication Manager, Kelly Tryba. Kelly worked with Hope House part time, as she also taught in the School of Journalism at the University of Colorado. Kelly was another team member who could have worked anywhere she chose for significantly more money than our little nonprofit could afford to pay her, but her years as a single mom had given her a deep sense of compassion for our girls, and she felt called to help them tell their stories.

Kelly and Lisa developed a communication campaign that included a one-page description featuring infographics, a simple way to break down our programs and describe how each one tackled a different aspect of generational poverty. Kelly began looking for new data as evidence of the girls' progress, which led the program team to start tracking all sorts of facts we hadn't previously tracked. Soon Jenny Macias determined that our current program database couldn't adequately pull the data Kelly had asked for and began searching for something more robust.

Another communication tool in place to this day was the development of an open house designed to walk our champions through the life of a teen mom as she worked toward self-sufficiency through our programs. Guests would arrive at the mini-Resource Center and be given a card with the background story of a typical teen mom.

As the tour moved through the building the guests would receive another card at each stop, each one bearing a description of the impact of the program area the teen mom had participated in. Although the previous cards were an amalgamation of the stories of our girls, the last stop featured a card with the real ending of the story of a teen mom who had been in our program for five years.

None of the responses we developed were quick fixes for the issues raised by that feasibility study. In fact, most would become part of a five-year strategic plan developed by our newest staff member, a semi-retired financial strategist, Gail Strobel. She was a realist about our finances and a stickler for pushing us to have better data.

Her pragmatic and measured planning process was the perfect balance to Jenny's heart, my impatience to see progress, and Lisa Schlarbaum's sense of urgency in all things. I am quite sure there were days when my drive to push things forward had her quite literally pulling out her hair, and while we were learning important lessons about communication with our champions we were also learning from Gail that we needed the operational foundation to support our planned growth.

What I had thought would be one year in our mini-Resource Center stretched into two and then three years as the preliminary development plan for the land had to be completed 100% through donated time and labor. While Lisa's team was growing our communication and fundraising strategies, Gail's tiny team developed new finance and operations procedures, including growing our HR and IT capabilities.

Meanwhile, under Jenny's leadership the program team had decided to abandon the Mentoring Program as a strategy for moving our moms to self-sufficiency, focusing their energy instead on each new program area the Mentoring Program had once represented.

In 2013 we formalized our new College & Career Program after rehiring Jamie Barnes, one of our first residential staff members who had taken a few years off to raise her babies. Ashley's GED Program had begun helping the girls fill out the FAFSA paperwork required to get a Pell grant so they could explore community college, something most of our teen moms didn't think was a possibility for them. Many of our girls were first-generation high school graduates, and *all* of them would be first-generation college students.

It didn't take long for us to realize that, though we could help get our moms into college, helping them stay there would be a whole different animal. Moms were dropping out, sometimes after only one semester, as they struggled with seemingly simple barriers, such as getting enough tutoring time and securing access to a computer and printer.

Jamie's background as an educator, coupled with her time as a residential team member, made her a perfect fit for the newly formed College & Career Program. She quickly built a volunteer tutoring program and set about getting donated laptops. Before we knew it we had fifteen moms in college, and those girls were bringing in more teen moms they had met on campus who were also struggling with a lack of access to tutors.

By 2014 we had turned the one room with a closing door in the mini-Resource Center into a childcare room as a response to the girls' need for babysitting while they studied for GED or college or participated in one of our parenting or healthy relationships classes. Jenny soon realized that we had an opportunity to provide more than just childcare, and our Early Learning Program was born with a curriculum designed to help our little ones start kindergarten school ready.

This new program would become the foundation of a new approach to all we do at Hope House, focusing on a two-generational model to breaking the cycle of poverty. The Early Learning Program began with a focus on literacy, aiming to combat the shocking national statistic that an adult in poverty typically has a working vocabulary of about nine hundred words, while a middle-class three-year-old has a working vocabulary of twelve hundred words.

It wouldn't be until 2015, after four annual phone calls to David Johnson, each to request one more year in his warehouse space, that the day finally came when our preliminary development plan was approved and we could formally purchase the land for our new building. That January day was cold, and a light snow was falling as Lisa and I drove through waning afternoon light to the title company offices. I wasn't sure that Christine Bess or Mindy Brown would make the drive north from their south suburban homes, but I shouldn't have worried. Neither of them was about to miss this historic moment for Hope House.

The four of us women, the church's realtor, the head of their trustee board, and the title officer crowded around the worn table in the overly warm office, and a pen was placed in my hand. I couldn't help but remember another day, many years earlier, when I had been alone in a similar office signing the loan papers that had led to a house for our teen moms, which had then led to our tiny warehouse and was now leading to a campus with a brand-new Resource Center.

As I put the pen to paper a collective whoop went up from our assembled crowd, and a historic day for Hope House ended, as usual, with hugs all around.

Janelle and the Arvada Mayor, Marc Williams, cutting the ribbon for the new resource center at the Grand Opening Ceremony, 2019

Pastor Tellis praying for the new resource center; the teen moms and children who will be empowered there; and the staff, volunteers, and champions that will support them, 2019

21

In Awe of What God Can Do

If God is for us, who can be against us?

ROMANS 8:31

I awoke on the day of the Grand Opening for our magnificent, 15,000-square-foot Resource Center with a million details for the celebration swirling in my head. It was a warm September morning in 2019, and the sun was splashed across the mountains to my west as I drove, etching the giant, dark blue and green peaks against a bright blue sky. Usually, a morning like this would draw a breath of wonder and whispered gratitude to God for allowing me to live in such a place as this.

Today all I could think of was the fact that the steel handrails on the steep side porch of the new building had been installed and painted just the day before. Would the paint be dry by the time the fire department came for the final occupancy inspection? The Grand Opening was slated to start at 4:00 p.m., and the fire department would be coming at 10:00

a.m. Talk about cutting it close! I parked in the church parking lot, knowing that we would soon be roping off our new parking lot for the big celebration.

All of the important people had been invited. Rusty Crandall, the president of our builder, Meritage Homes, would be there, along with Glenn Nier and his team, who had worked tirelessly for almost three years to build this building. HomeAid Colorado, a nonprofit dedicated to bringing builders together to assist those working to eradicate homelessness, would come, having taken us on as their first commercial building project— and what an adventure that had turned out to be!

Steve Prokopiak, our faithful board member and building committee chair, had invested close to forty hours a week on leading this project to completion, along with our architect, Jeanne Fielding, and our volunteer project manager, Angie Gibbs. The project had spanned three board chair tenures, from Mindy Brown to Brandon Ideker to Brian Bess, all of whom had provided invaluable leadership. This day wouldn't be happening without them and so many others.

The mayor would be there to cut the ribbon, and the local media was supposed to cover the event. Most importantly, our amazing champions and teen moms were coming to celebrate together—the girls whose lives God was changing and the people He had called to provide them with this amazing new building to call their own.

Lisa Schlarbaum and her team would end up spending a total of four years raising the funds for this building, as I had already spent four years working alongside Steve and Meritage Homes to see it built. It had been an incredibly long and tiring journey, with many bumps along the way, but all of the difficulties and weariness seemed to have evaporated into the warm fall air on this historic day.

I hurried across the lot to the north door, still marveling that I could open the big outside door with the swipe of my key card across the blinking little box on the side of the building. The lock opened with a satisfying click, and I pushed through the door, balancing bouquets of flowers for the front reception desk and my cup of coffee. The building still smelled so new, like drywall dust and fresh paint.

Every surface in the building gleamed. Our staff had spent days cleaning it, often joined by current teen moms and alumni. The day before had been particularly hot as we ran vacuums, wiped dusty surfaces, and removed leftover bits of blue painter's tape.

I smiled to myself as I recalled how Kelly Tryba had brought banana popsicles and stored them in the walk-in freezer (we had a walk-in freezer!) and then promptly shooed us all outside to eat them because she didn't want drips on the new dining room floor. Alondra had taken the day off from Children's Hospital, where she was now a nurse, to help with the cleaning, and it made my heart smile to watch our now-grown-up girl laugh and joke with the staff as we cleaned.

The staff wouldn't actually move in until the following day. The boxes were packed at the old building, stacked to the ceiling in that tiny space, and the battered old office cubicles had been dismantled and thrown away. Here, the desks stood in gleaming white rows against brand new cubicle walls in a neutral tan shade. Each workstation had an overhead bin, an expensive desk chair, a purple accent wall board for hanging things, and a file cabinet that rolled out from under the desk and was covered with a lime green padding on top so that a teen mom could pull it out and sit at the desk while chatting with a staff member.

The dark tiled floors gleamed. I marveled that luxury vinyl tile could look so much like hardwood. Along the front of the building a huge bank of windows let the morning sunshine pour in, filling the office area with light all the way to the crest of the vaulted ceiling and bouncing off the eggplant-colored accent wall in the main reception area.

Brand new commercial-grade furniture filled the space, from lime-green and gray armchairs to gleaming white stand-up desks, all courtesy of Doris, a beautiful Hope House champion whom I had never even met. Doris was in her eighties and lived in California. She had made an incredibly generous gift upon the advice of her philanthropic advisors at Excellence in Giving.

They had shared with her a video of Janelle telling her story at one of our golf tournaments. Doris had been moved by Janelle and wanted her gift designated for brand new furniture, because that was what she felt the girls deserved. As I took in the beautifully furnished reception area, I couldn't have agreed more.

I laid my armful of flowers on the granite top of the reception desk, breathing a sigh of relief that it had been installed three days earlier, finally replacing the plywood version. The new chairs in the reception area were lime green and gray, and the round white accent tables matched the desks.

Lisa Schlarbaum, who had an eye for design hidden beneath her fierce fundraising skills, had adorned the tables with perfectly arranged pale pink silk flower arrangements. All of the interior design work had been chosen or approved by Lisa, and although I had been initially unsure about the bright white and splashes of lime green, I had to admit that the building looked beautiful. The mamas were going to love it, and I couldn't wait to show it off.

The doorbell inside the front vestibule buzzed, and I pushed open one of the double glass doors to allow Steve Prokopiak to enter. A big guy with a commanding presence, Steve was a retired civil engineer, and he had single-handedly spearheaded the construction of this building. He was here to meet the fire department for the final inspection, and he was in no-nonsense mode, ready to rush the presumed approval to the building inspector so we could get our final certificate of occupancy. Steve could be a bit intimidating, which wasn't all bad when he had to get a crew of subs to move it along during construction. I knew he had a marshmallow heart, though, especially when it came to our teen moms and their struggles.

Right behind the fire inspector our staff began arriving, sporting their brand-new Hope House logo t-shirts and excited to get set up for our grand opening. We had borrowed a small stage from the church next door and even had a red carpet to roll out for the mayor, builders, and special guests. We had roped off the front lot and set up signs directing cars to the church parking lot next door. We were expecting close to 250 people, and parking would be tight. By 2:30 p.m., with only an hour to spare before the sneak peek for our major donors, we had received our certificate of occupancy (whew!).

The Bess family and the Idekers were the first to arrive, and both Brian and Doug teared up as they entered through the sparkling glass vestibule into the spacious reception area. Gail Coors, the Gryzmala family, and the Houglands arrived, and as Lisa began to lead them on a quick private tour you could feel the joy in the air.

I was excited to see Wes and Allyson Gardner arrive, and right behind them Bill and Donna Wehner. Wes had been such a blessing through the years, developing our first attempt at a career program by matching teen moms with jobs in his company and engaging other business owners to do the same.

Donna Wehner had been writing stories for us for years, always interviewing our mamas with so much grace and empathy, and Bill had shared his business prowess and advice with me on many occasions.

Bill was one of the advisors whom I always wanted to make proud. I was honored to lead them on a quick tour before I ducked outside to check on setup. In fifteen minutes the celebration would begin, and staff was just finishing stretching a purple ribbon from one end of the building to the other. Cars were beginning to arrive.

I glanced nervously at my watch. John wasn't there yet, and I hoped he would be able to find a parking spot. People were beginning to fill up the front lot, happily ignoring the light, misty rain that had begun to fall. I hurried back inside to make sure our preview guests were ready to come back outside for the opening remarks. Distracted and decidedly nervous, I almost bumped right into my sweet Bible study girls lined up by the reception desk. Someone had snuck them in so they could surprise me before the festivities began.

I burst into what would be the first of many happy tears that day as they surrounded me, squishing balloons and flowers into a group hug. The group consisted of seven beautiful ladies whom I never would have met had it not been for Hope House, some of our very first donors and the most faith-filled friends who had prayed, listened, and generally encouraged me all the way through the Hope House journey to this celebration day. My heart filled with gratitude for each one: Laurie, Jackie, Terrie, Tami, Carolyn, Lindy, and Lori. After the quick group hug they pushed me out through the front vestibule to greet the local news anchor who had arrived to emcee.

The parking lot had completely filled up with people, a bright swirl of women in colorful summer dresses and men in slacks, all dressed up for the occasion and mostly uncaring that the light rain was dampening their clothes. I finally found John off to my right with our longtime board member Pastor John Tellis, who would open the event in prayer.

I would learn later that they had barely made it before the 4:30 p.m. start time because they'd had to park way up the street. The church parking lot had filled completely, and guests were still trekking in from surrounding neighborhoods, some four hundred people in all!

Pastor John stepped up to the microphone and welcomed the crowd, who fell into a hushed silence as his booming voice invited everyone to bow for prayer. As always, the power of his deep voice, the Southern drawl, and the cadence of his prayer captivated us all. As he thanked God for each person present; each contributor to this day; and most importantly, each teen mom and child God was entrusting to our care, the air filled with emotion, and spontaneous clapping began. I'm pretty sure this wasn't the first time people had responded with applause to this Baptist preacher's powerful prayers.

Pastor John introduced Rusty Crandall from Meritage, who shared what an honor it had been for their whole company to have been the builder on this project, and Cindy Bell echoed the sentiment on behalf of HomeAid. Then, suddenly, the mic was being handed to me, and I realized as I stepped up onto our little stage that I hadn't even prepared any remarks.

I panicked for a second, looking out into what seemed a sea of people. My eyes locked with those of one of our Hope House alumni, Alex, who had her arms around the shoulders of her now five-year-old twins, and I felt a sense of pure joy welling up inside me. I began to thank the crowd, the individual contributors, and our amazing board.

Then I turned my head and caught John's eye and, knowing he would be all kinds of embarrassed, asked him to come stand next to me. My voice cracked as I shared how this day, indeed Hope House in general, would never have come to be if it hadn't been for the love, support, and wisdom of this man.

Then I searched for Lisa Schlarbaum and, knowing she would be all kinds of annoyed at the attention, called her to stand at my other side. I thanked her for her leadership, relationship building, and passion for empowering our teen moms that had made this campus possible.

Because of her relentless commitment, and because of the incredible generosity of the people we stood with today, this building was being opened 100% debt free. In the end Lisa and her team had raised $5.4 million in cash and in-kind contributions for this building, while also growing our annual operating budget by double digits each year, all while ensuring that each champion had an opportunity to experience God through their giving.

Standing there with John and Lisa, I could feel my throat getting tight and my eyes prickling with tears. I wrapped up with a prayer of thanks to the One ultimately responsible for this amazing day, the God Who loves our girls beyond all that they can think or imagine. He had built this building just for them, a place to be safe from judgment, a place to be loved, a place to belong. Finally, with a wave of my hand at the beautiful building behind me, I said the only thing left to say: "Just look what God can do!"

With that our mayor stepped forward and invited Janelle to join him. Since that long ago night stuck in her car in a snowstorm, this young woman had gone on to finish a degree in applied science and had become a machinist at Ball Aerospace. Today this happily married girl, whose youth had been marked by homelessness, was a proud homeowner.

Janelle grasped the handles of the giant ceremonial scissors and, with a flourish and a huge grin, cut the purple ribbon, while the entire crowd erupted into cheers and applause. At just that moment, as if God had planned it all along, the misty rain stopped, and warm yellow rays of sunshine broke through the clouds and fell across the cheering crowd.

Brittany with her daughters, Anahlei (left) and Arianna (right), 2009

Megan with her sons, Tristan (left) and Ben (right), 2013

22

Real Change Happens Only in Relationship

I will give thanks to you, LORD, with all my heart;
I will tell of all of your wonderful deeds.

PSALM 9:1

On a recent Friday afternoon our Housing Support Program Manager knocked on the doorframe of my office in the Resource Center. Sliding into the cute green chair in my sun-filled office, Brittany shared how hard her day had been. She had led the decision-making team who interviewed and approved potential residents, and with 250 teen moms participating in our programs each year, these decisions could be excruciating. Today had been one of those days.

Part of the aftermath of COVID had been a huge surge in the number of teen moms experiencing homelessness. Our residential house was at capacity, and it had broken Brittany's heart to have to turn away a nineteen-year-old mom with a one-year-old son who had recently lost her housing because she had allowed her two elementary school-aged siblings to move into her section-8 housing after her mom had abandoned them. The neighbors had called the housing authority, who had promptly kicked them all out. She desperately wanted to help this girl, but the best she could offer were hotel vouchers.

Brittany's lip trembled as she told me the story. Then she took a deep breath, wiped her eyes, and said, "You know, I just had to go home last night and hand this situation back to Him. God gave this mama a place to do her laundry, eat a meal, and feel safe and loved on for a few hours. But He knew when He brought her through the doors of the Resource Center that the house was already full. Which means that He already had a plan in place for her living situation. My decision wasn't the last stop in God's plan."

I sat back in my chair and marveled at Brittany. Barely thirty years old and full of such deep faith and wisdom. Brittany made *me* feel better about a difficult situation. She reminded me that we aren't here to rescue our girls at any cost but to use the tools we do have available to us in any given situation.

It struck me while we talked how incredible it was that God had brought Brittany, like many of our former teen moms, full circle from program participants to staff members, board members, volunteers, and donors. I remembered visiting Brittany in the tiny house in central Denver where she had once lived. I had noticed that the living room window was cracked, and Brittany had pointed to the bullet hole where the window had been pierced in a drive-by shooting that had fortunately happened while no one was home.

She had lived with various abusive family members and in a group home before moving into Hope House at seventeen, with two-year-old Anahlei and baby Ari in tow. Even then Brittany was a calm, patient mama with a quiet determination that only occasionally came out as stubbornness.

Brittany, like most of our teen moms—like *me*—would once have been considered the *least* likely to do amazing things. Yet we had somehow been chosen by God to not only be a part of Hope House but to be leaders. I knew that God had historically chosen unlikely people to lead.

For example, Moses was reluctant, prone to angry outbursts, and needed his brother to do his public speaking for him; Paul was initially a violent persecutor of Christians; Peter was just a common fisherman, and not a very good one at that; and Mary, an unmarried teenage girl, was chosen to carry Jesus, God's own Son. In my head I know that God chooses flawed and ordinary people for leadership. Yet in my heart, if I am honest, I often question whether God really knew what He was doing when He chose me to be the founder and leader of Hope House.

In the course of my work, people will often ask me about my background. They expect me to say that I have a master's degree in such-and-such, have worked in human services, was an educator, or to delineate any number of other professional accomplishments. Instead, I tell them that I am a former teen mom who grew up in a chaotic home, got married at seventeen, never went to college, and worked as a home daycare provider.

When I give that answer, sitting in my office in our beautiful Resource Center surrounded by busy staff working with classrooms full of teen moms and children, I invariably get a look of amazement, or even disbelief, followed by, "Wow! How did you do this?"

Every time my answer is, "In all honesty, *I* didn't."

I get to point to Him because there simply is no other answer, not because I want to preach or persuade. I get to share how God has surrounded me, and our teen moms, with the most amazing people throughout the years. Even more extraordinary is how many have stayed involved in the long term, like the elderly Petits, who started giving $5.00 a month before we had even opened the doors and twenty years later still makes a monthly gift (now $15.00).

Sharron Neufeld no longer leads the prayer team, a group of over one hundred today, but she has made it her mission to pray regularly for every single staff member. Clarene Shelley has long since retired from policing and from our board, but today she brings her deep faith and experience to our staff as our workplace chaplain.

When Betty turned eighty we held a surprise birthday party, the only kind we could throw her, since she would have pitched a fit if we'd given her undue attention. She got her second surprise party just a few months ago when she turned ninety. Betty started volunteering at Hope House after she and her husband had sold their drywall business. She had helped us with bookkeeping and filing and still comes in weekly, doing whatever odd jobs we may have for her. We once presented Betty with a six-foot-long chart that looked like an enormous family tree.

At the top of the chart were Betty and Bill, a World War II vet who had a crusty exterior but a marshmallow heart. Below them were Betty's children, Terrie & Doug Ideker, and below them John and Laurie Scott, followed by a whole group of people John had brought to us while he was chairman of the board.

John had taught me early on about the power of connectedness and inclusion and about how God weaves people together for a common purpose. What we wanted Betty to see through her family tree was how one "little old lady," as she calls herself, could make such an enormous impact. Every person she had introduced to Hope House had introduced another, and that one another yet, until the branches had grown too numerous to fit onto our paper tree.

In our very early days Gerideane had come to volunteer, doing light office work. One afternoon she overheard me on the phone with our insurance broker, frustrated with myself because I couldn't fully grasp the complicated employee benefits language. Gerideane asked if she could help, and I shrugged her off, unsure how this retiree could help me.

Thankfully, Gerideane persisted. It turns out that she had spent her career in the benefits field, and she knew exactly what the broker had been talking about. For the next five years Gerideane oversaw our insurance and benefits, all as a volunteer, and I learned an important lesson in the process: never underestimate the power of the volunteer!

Marv and Tom were regulars at Hope House. They had become fast friends, and both had keys to Hope House. Every week you could find them repairing a fence, painting a wall, or fixing a squeaky door. The two of them were the unofficial "men of the house," and we loved them to pieces, even though they were both long winded when they stopped by to chat after having completed a project.

By the time Marv was diagnosed with Alzheimer's, he had spent fifteen years mowing our lawn, patching our brick, playing Santa Claus at Christmas, and aerating neighborhood lawns in order to raise money for us. Marv no longer recognizes most of our faces, but he still knows Hope House when he sees the building. During the pandemic his caregiver would drive him through the parking lot in her van, and the staff and mamas would stand on either side of the drive to whoop and cheer and wave hand-painted signs that read "We Love You, Marv." Marv would light up every time.

As the self-appointed "guardian of the ice melt," Tom had made sure our buckets of the solution never ran out in the winter. The year there was a shortage in the ice melt supply, Tom drove back East for a family reunion. He returned two weeks later with three fifty-pound bags of ice melt roped to his roof, and a wife who was as mad as a wet hen about how much longer the trip had taken with all that weight slowing them down.

Tom's weekly visits for coffee and donuts slowed down as the years went by, until his last visit in the new Resource Center building, where he sat back in a dining room chair, cane by his side, and shared stories of the "old days" with the new staff. Tom passed away at ninety, and our Hope House community filled a row at his service.

Hope House is just like that. God draws people to us. These champions often give money or volunteer time, but more importantly, they make up the fabric of our family. Most of our girls have never before experienced a safe, loving, laughter-filled community. They crave it. They are drawn into this place and the people God has filled it with.

Our beautiful Resource Center is 15,000 square feet of *home* to our mamas, and the people who fill the rooms are like family to them. They know that when they celebrate their GED graduation, Rosi will bake them the most beautiful cake creation they have ever seen. They know that Rita will bring in breakfast and that Steve, Gene, and Jeff will be present, faithfully working on household projects. The GED girls come into the Learning Lab knowing that Sandy, Craig, and Donna will be there to help with homework and that Kim, Sandy, and Sheri will be sorting donated clothes and household goods for them.

The then two-year old Darrien may have said it best years ago when I was walking through the living room one day and tripped on a piece of carpet trim that needed to be nailed down again. From his highchair in the dining room, he watched me catch myself and shouted his encouragement, his *r*s sounding like *w*s, as usual: "Don't wowwy! Mawv will fix it!"

Jamie and her son, Darrien, 2010

Teen moms with their firstborn—representing each year of Hope House's history—on stage at the 20th Anniversary Hope House Colorado Gala, 2022

23

The Challenge to Say Yes to God

Walk in the way of love.

EPHESIANS 5:2

The night of our Twentieth Anniversary Gala was cool and clear. Guests dressed in formal finery, from suits and jackets to sequined gowns, poured into the lobby of the downtown Denver hotel, ready to celebrate twenty years of God's provision for Hope House Colorado. I greeted guests with hugs and smiles, ever excited to be with our champions, but my heart leapt for our beautiful girls, now arriving with Jamie Barnes, our Empower Program Manager and faithful stalwart for our mamas.

Our program graduates for the year are invited to attend the gala in recognition of their hard work to reach self-sufficiency. Weeks before the event they attend Boutique Night, getting to choose a donated gown from among the racks at a local nonprofit. The staff ooh and ahh and ask them to turn in swirling circles as they choose just the right dress—almost always a long gown enhanced by glittery jeweled earrings and too-high heels, and occasionally even a tiara. Tonight the mamas look as if they've stepped straight out of a Hollywood awards show. Their smiles are contagious.

The air is filled with a sense of expectation as 450 guests flow into the ballroom, where tables are set with linens and silver, glassware glitters, and the air is filled with the delicious smells of the meal about to be served. The lights begin to dim as I settle at a table in the front of the room with Gary Corbett, our forever-auctioneer; Dave Runyon, our emcee and greatest cheerleader; and most importantly, my husband and now adult children and my son-in-law.

The room grows quiet as the video fills the large screens in this giant ballroom. It's a beautiful ode to Hope House's twenty years of existence, filled with stories of our growth as a ministry, funny pictures of John and me getting married as teenagers, me in braces and he in an eighties mullet, and the long-ago donated house with the brick torn off.

As the video ends, I stand and begin moving toward the stage. I chose a long, velvety, burgundy-colored gown, the first time I've worn a long dress in twenty years of gala speeches, but I wanted to fit right in with our mamas tonight. I draw a deep breath as I reach the stage stairs and remind God, as I always do, that I need Him to give me breath if He wants me to speak past the nerves and excitement of this moment.

When I reach the microphone I am filled with both peace and a sense of the surreal. The room is full of so many dear champions, now lifelong friends. All of my wise advisors; my pastor, John Tellis; my co-founder, Amie Walton; and my two amazing sisters who have traveled across the country to be here.

Staff and former staff are also present, along with current and past board members, donors who have been faithfully giving for twenty straight years, and brand-new donors who are about to become part of something momentous. Yet twenty seats across the immense ballroom are conspicuously empty as I begin speaking to our assembled guests.

"Sometimes I think that we have heard the term 'breaking the cycle' so many times that it has lost some of its meaning. We talk about poverty and self-sufficiency in sweeping terms, forgetting how hard it is to *actually* break the cycle of poverty for two generations. Tonight I get to introduce you to the astounding young women who have done just that."

As the music comes up, a door near the back of the room opens, and a long line of my personal superheroes enters the ballroom, led by my son Johnny. He has a commanding presence at 6'3", dressed in his formal suit; he's now a grown man married to a beautiful woman, Ashley, and daddy to three precious girls who hold my heart in their little hands. Behind him walk Fendia and her daughter, Sarah; then Tabitha and Lorena; Brittany and Anahlei, and on down to the newest of our teen moms, Mekhi, with her baby boy, Lucas.

The room is hushed as all twenty pairs of moms and children fill the stage and I hand the microphone to my son Johnny.

"Hi, I'm Johnny Steven, and I am here tonight to tell my parents that I am proud of them. I couldn't have had better parents, who are an example for my wife and me of what marriage can look like and an example of following God when He calls you to do something big."

Johnny hands the microphone to Fendia, and with her still lilting Creole accent she says, "I am Fendia. I was the first resident of Hope House. Today I am a managing nurse at an assisted living facility, and my husband and I have an additional daughter and own our own home."

Fendia hands the microphone to Sarah, who speaks with her own musical lilt, "I'm Sarah, and I am nineteen years old. I am studying at Metro State University to become a psychiatric nurse."

Sarah hands the microphone to the tiny woman next to her, Tabitha. The second graduate from Hope House, Tabitha came to us with only a third-grade reading level. Still shy, Tabitha softly shares her name and explains that she has had a long career as a hair stylist and that she and her husband now have three children, before handing the microphone to her daughter Lorena.

"I'm Lorena, and I'm eighteen and graduating high school in May. I have straight *As* and a scholarship to go to college, where I plan to study medicine."

Lorena hands the microphone to Brittany, who shares that she is a Hope House graduate and a married mother of five and is also our Housing Support Program Manager at Hope House. Brittany hands the microphone to her stunning daughter, Anahlei, now taller than her mom.

"I'm Anahlei. I'm seventeen years old. I'm a junior in high school and plan to attend college on a volleyball scholarship."

After each one speaks, there is a burst of applause from the audience, now all on their feet in the longest standing ovation in gala history. The microphone passes to each mom and child. Megan, who was a terrified eighteen-year-old who had been threatened with the loss of her son when she moved into Hope House, is now a college graduate and our Housing Navigator at Hope House; she understands our girls' housing crisis on a personal level. Her son, Tristan, that once spiky-haired two-year-old, now towers over his mom, wearing his first suit jacket and a paisley tie that he picked out especially to match his mom's dress.

Jamie, who dropped out at fifteen, takes the mic from Tristan and shares that she is now going to college and studying engineering. Her son, Darrien, a high school sophomore, shares that he is a football player and a great dog sitter (mine).

Marisa, my tiny spitfire, has to reach up to take the mic from Darrien; she shares that she is now the married mother of four and was recently promoted to supervisor in her role with Denver Human Services. Neesy, dressed in a golden gown that makes her look much older than her fourteen years, takes the microphone and shyly shares her dreams of the future.

Each mom shares her dreams and hands the microphone to her child, on down to Rosalena and her four-year-old son, who proudly shares that he wants to work at Target when he grows up.

This night represents the culmination of twenty years of watching God move in incredible ways, often questioning my own abilities but never my "why." Twenty years of learning how to lead, often painfully but with always hard-learned humbleness and curiosity. Twenty years of watching teen moms like these beautiful women standing on stage with me break down every barrier to self-sufficiency, turn every stereotype and statistic on its head, and build stable and healthy lives for their children— truly breaking the cycle of poverty for every generation to follow.

Somewhere out there a teen mama is curled up in a ball around her tiny newborn, terrified and isolated but determined to provide a better life for her baby than what she has known. At that same instant God is gently whispering to her, "Just hold on, I'm sending my people."

Twenty years in, and God is not finished with Hope House. This year we will open a new Early Learning Center on our campus, providing full-time childcare to over one hundred children of our teen moms. Our affiliate program is just gathering steam, partnering with Colleen Emery to open our first affiliate in northern Colorado, affectionately known as Hope House NoCO; with Amanda Kolman, the executive director of Hope House Cañon City in the southern part of our state; and with Myrna Bittar, our first out-of-state affiliate opening Hope House Orange County, California.

Our Director of Partnerships is developing training modules, partner workshops, and coaching paths for women across the country who feel called to open a Hope House for teen moms in their communities. These women, so like me, are hair stylists, pastors' wives, Young Lives leaders, and retail clerks. They don't feel qualified, but then, God so often chooses those least qualified to do the most amazing things.

All you have to do, after all, is say yes.

Hope House Colorado's campus is located in Arvada, Colorado. The campus includes a resource center (foreground) that opened in 2019, a residential house (located just right of the resource center) that has provided safe housing for over 100 teen moms and their children since 2003, and an early learning center (located behind the resource center). The early learning center is set to open in August 2024 and will provide quality, licensed child care for up to 104 children of teen moms and staff at Hope House.

HOPE ♥ HOUSE
COLORADO

Hope House Colorado empowers parenting teenage moms to strive for personal and economic self-sufficiency and to understand their significance in God's sight, resulting in a healthy future for them and for their children.

Hope House provides free self-sufficiency programs to parenting teen moms in three key areas. The Empower Program provides opportunities for personal, educational and economic self-sufficiency for teen moms. This includes educational assistance through High School & GED and College & Career Programs. Additional supportive services include healthy relationships and personal growth classes, licensed counseling, legal advocacy and financial literacy. The Housing Support Program provides metro-Denver's only Residential Program for teen moms, and additional housing supports through various partnerships. The Early Learning & School Age Program focuses on literacy and social-emotional development; early intervention services; and school-age supports for the children; and provides a Parenting Program. All programs are designed to transform the lives of two generations at Hope House. Hope House relies on numerous volunteers and local business partnerships to accomplish its mission.

To learn more about Hope House Colorado, visit www.hopehousecolorado.org.

Follow Hope House Colorado on social media:

f Hope House Colorado   **◯** @hopehousecolorado

in Hope House Colorado

To learn more about becoming a Hope House affiliate, please email expansion@hopehousecolorado.org.

www.ingramcontent.com/pod-product-compliance
Lightning Source LLC
Chambersburg PA
CBHW062050080426

42734CB00012B/2604